COMPETITION, REGULATION, AND RATIONING
IN HEALTH CARE

COMPETITION, REGULATION, AND RATIONING IN HEALTH CARE

Warren Greenberg

Health Administration Press
Ann Arbor, Michigan 1991

95 94 93 92 91 5 4 3 2 1

Library of Congress Cataloging-in-Publication Data

Greenberg, Warren.
Competition, regulation, and rationing in health care / Warren Greenberg.
p. cm.
Includes biographical references and index.
ISBN 0-910701-77-6 (hardbound : alk. paper)
1. Medical economics—United States. 2. Medical care—Law and legislation—United States. 3. Competition—United States. 4. Rationing, Consumer—United States. I. Title
[DNLM: 1. Delivery of Health Care—economics—United States. 2. Economic Competition. 3. Facility Regulation and Control—United States. 4. Health Care Rationing. W 84 AA1 G79c]
RA410.53G74 1991 338/4'73621'0973—dc20
DNLM/DLC for Library of Congress 91-35326 CIP

The paper used in this publication meets the minimum requirements of American National Standard for Information Sciences—Permanence of Paper for Printed Library Materials, ANSI Z39.48-1984. ♾™

Health Administration Press
A division of the Foundation of the
American College of Healthcare Executives
1021 East Huron Street
Ann Arbor, Michigan 48104-9990
(313) 764-1380

To Judith and Elyssa

Contents

Preface

This book provides an economist's view of the health care sector. Since I began studying the health care economy in 1975, the amount of resources devoted to health care in the United States has grown from $133 billion and 8.5 percent of the gross national product to $671 billion and 12.2 percent of the gross national product (in 1990). This rapid increase—in both absolute and relative terms—in health care expenditures is often greeted with scorn and unease by the American public. In contrast, increases of this magnitude in sales or expenditures for commodities such as new automobiles or videocassette recorders would bring smiles to the faces of newscasters and citizens throughout the country. One of my main tasks, therefore, was to set out why the health care sector may be analyzed differently from other industries. To this end, I have attempted to convey in this book the forces of competition, regulation, and rationing that best describe the health care sector, and to provide a glimpse of what changes may occur in the future.

I have written this book from the standpoint of an industrial organization economist—an economist who analyzes an industry's attributes (such as the degree of competition and regulation) and its conduct (such as pricing behavior or advertising). I have found industrial organization economics, a specialized branch of microeconomics, to be essential in analyzing current industry performance and valuable in predicting performance in the future. Those who say that the health care sector is unique and cannot be analyzed by industrial organization economics might be amused to know that representatives from the petroleum, cereal, and automobile industries all made similar assertions to me at the Federal Trade Commission (FTC) when I was staff economist there. Each industry, including health care, may have some unique attributes, but all can be analyzed using the same industrial organization techniques.

This book is suitable for the informed layperson who is interested in the workings of the health care sector and does not mind reading a book with footnotes. It is also suitable for the student of health economics who does not mind reading a text without mathematical equations.

I have attempted to write this book without bias, but it is possible that some biases will appear. I am skeptical of government regulation (due to my experiences with government and my reading of the academic literature), but I have found that the proposed Dutch health care system, due to be implemented in 1995, is the least regulatory and the most equitable system of which I am aware. Elimination of employer-based health insurance would be a needed first step in importing the proposed Dutch system, or its variant, in the United States.

I have attempted to identify and describe the most essential elements of the physician, hospital, insurance, and long-term care industries. The book explores why and how each of these industries may be different from the shoe or automobile industry, for example, and describes the market failures or imperfections in each industry. It also includes an examination of some of the avenues that government has taken to correct these imperfections. At the end of the book, I have presented a review of the British, Canadian, and Dutch systems to ascertain what lessons the United States may be able to learn from these countries.

Many have suggested that the U.S. health care system is in a crisis. This book should enable us to understand the system a little better and will encourage students, researchers, managers, professionals, and policymakers to continue the search for a more efficient and equitable health care system. Whatever the components of that system may be, I am convinced that doses of competition, regulation, and rationing will be necessary.

I would like to thank Professor Wynand van de Ven and other reviewers for their helpful comments regarding the manuscript. The book has also benefited from the comments of Deborah Kamin and my conversations over the years with David Kass, Bob Helms, and Lawrence Goldberg. I would also like to thank my research assistants: Lisa Openshaw, Elizabeth Kurtz, Lisa Buono, Lauren Mobley, Harold de Weese, Hui Tzu, and Iman Copty. I extend a special thank-you to Syed Hossain for his word processing and computer assistance. I also learned (tuition-free) from my health economics students at George

Washington over the last nine years about the areas that are most meaningful to them in their academic study of this subject.

I thank also Nancy Moncrieff, who works with Health Administration Press, for her conscientious editing and encouragement throughout the writing of this book. She held me to her own high standards in this endeavor. Deborah Glazer also made a number of valuable editorial suggestions earlier on in the process.

Finally, I thank the economists, health policy analysts, policymakers, and librarians who make Washington, D.C., the health care capital of the world in terms of its human and physical resources.

As is customary, I bear full responsibility for this book, but I claim only small responsibility for any changes that may occur in health care policy after its publication.

1

Introduction to the Economics of Health Care

What is the appropriate mix of competition and regulation in the provision of health care? Will rationing be necessary in health care, and what form might it take? What is the best way to allocate resources in this sector? What is the appropriate balance of efficiency and equity? What role might government play? What are the differences, if any, between nonprofit and for-profit firms? Is health care a business?

Economics, or more particularly industrial organization microeconomics, can be a powerful tool in understanding the behavior and subsequent performance of firms and industries in the U.S. economy. It will also be of substantial help in understanding the health care sector.

The aim of this book is twofold. First, it is to provide an understanding of how the health care sector works. In a time of unprecedented change in this sector, economic analysis can help separate myth from fact; it can help suggest which changes and trends are desirable and which may be deleterious. Economic analysis can tell us whether or not shifts to more competition in this sector can help contain rising health care costs, can improve distribution of health services to the indigent, or can improve the quality of care. Most important of all, economics can help one appreciate the trade-offs that must be made in achieving a desired health system or policy.

The second aim of this book is a policy-oriented one. It suggests that a competitive climate in health care, although mostly desirable, involves serious limitations in the distribution of health services. An injection of government regulation, subsidies, and incentives will be necessary. Moreover, this book suggests that a competitive system will not preclude a shift to increased rationing of health care.

Industrial organization microeconomics has provided valuable insights on the shift from regulation to deregulation in industries outside health care. Economic analysis, for example, predicted that increased entry of new airlines and reduced prices on many routes would occur after price regulation, and limits on entry were removed in that industry. Economic analysis also predicted the failure of some existing airlines and the abandonment of unprofitable routes. In another example, economists predicted the increase as well as the variety of interest rates paid by banks for demand deposits as a result of deregulation in the banking industry.

In this chapter, I will describe the size and scope of the health care sector. I will ask if and how this sector differs from other industries or sectors; that is, does the health care sector respond in ways similar to other sectors to the forces of supply and demand? I will explain why most economists believe that competition will allocate resources, including health care resources, most efficiently; but I will show that competitive markets (including health care) can be imperfect and explain why government intervention and rationing may be necessary.

Size and Scope of the Health Care Sector

The health care sector, both in terms of number of employees and amount of total revenues, is the third largest sector in the economy, after agriculture and construction. It is larger, for example, than the transportation and computer sectors combined.

A sector comprises many industries that are related in terms of production or distribution but do not compete directly with one another. For example, the pharmaceutical and nursing home industries are both considered to be within the health care sector, yet there is little competition between the two. An industry, in contrast, such as acute care hospitals, is a group of firms that may compete against one another. Table 1.1 shows national expenditures for the various industries that constitute the health care sector.

A striking aspect of the health care sector is that the absolute dollar amount of expenditures and the percentage of gross national product (GNP) devoted to this sector have been increasing at a rapid pace (Table 1.2).

This rapid increase in expenditures in the health care sector does not necessarily imply that there are economic imperfections in the way that health care is delivered, but it could be a symptom of an

Table 1.1 National Expenditures for Health Care Sector Industries, 1985–1988

Industry	*Yearly Expenditure in Billions of Dollars*			
	1985	*1986*	*1987*	*1988*
Hospital care	167.9	179.3	193.7	211.8
Physician services	74.0	82.1	93.0	105.1
Drugs and other medical nondurables	32.3	35.6	38.6	41.9
Nursing home care	34.1	36.7	39.7	43.1
Other professional services	16.6	18.3	20.2	22.5
Other health care expenditures	95.2	98.5	103.6	115.5
Total health care sector	420.1	450.5	488.8	539.9

Source: Health Care Financing Administration, Office of National Cost Estimates (1990). "National Health Care Expenditures, 1988," *Health Care Financing Review* 11: 25.

Table 1.2 National Health Care Expenditures and Gross National Product, 1960–1988

Year	*Expenditure in Billions of Dollars*	*GNP in Billions of Dollars*	*Percentage of GNP*
1960	27.1	515	5.3
1965	41.6	705	5.9
1970	74.4	1,015	7.3
1975	132.9	1,598	8.3
1980	249.1	2,732	9.1
1985	420.1	4,015	10.5
1986	450.5	4,232	10.6
1987	488.8	4,524	10.8
1988	539.9	4,881	11.1

Source: Health Care Financing Administration, Office of National Cost Estimates (1990). "National Health Care Expenditures, 1988," *Health Care Financing Review* 11: 24.

underlying problem. I will discuss rising health care expenditures more fully in Chapter 10.

The health care sector is larger and growing faster than most sectors of the economy, but how susceptible is it to economic analysis? Although the health care sector is unique in the sense that it consists of a set of goods and services not sold in other sectors, each sector or industry in the economy can be characterized in this way. The real issue here is the extent to which attributes of the health care sector make it impervious to the tools of economics.

The main tools of economic analysis are built on supply and demand curves that are applicable to the supply and demand for all goods and services within and outside the health care sector (Figure 1.1). The upward-sloping supply curve (s–s) shows the amount of goods or

Figure 1.1 Market Demand and Market Supply

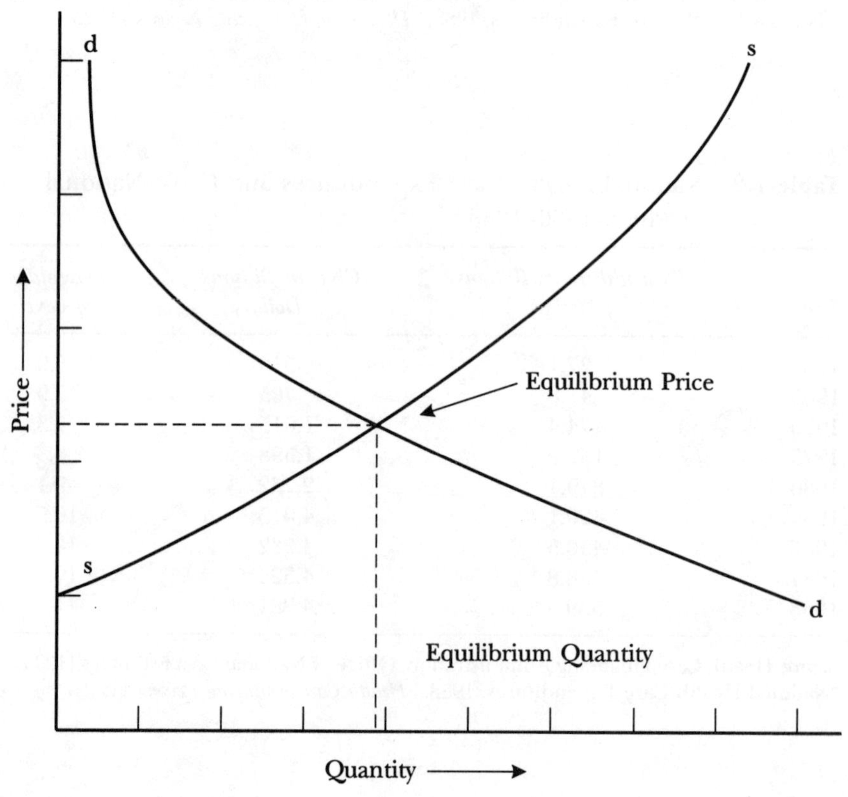

services that sellers are willing to supply at a set of possible prices. The higher the price of a good or service, the greater the quantity that the seller is willing to supply and offer for sale.

The downward-sloping demand curve (d–d) shows the quantities of goods or services that are demanded at a set of possible prices. The lower the price of a good or service, the greater the quantity that the buyer is willing to demand.

The intersection of the supply and demand curves will establish the actual equilibrium price at which the good or service will be sold. At a hypothesized price below this equilibrium level, the quantity demanded will exceed the quantity supplied, which will put upward pressure on price. At a hypothesized price above the equilibrium level, quantity supplied will exceed quantity demanded, which will put downward pressure on price. Throughout this book, we shall refer to the supply and demand for health care goods and services, which will often illustrate the explanatory power of these two curves.

Economists have isolated two potential differences between health care and other sectors of the economy, although even these are subject to dispute among experts. These differences are the uncertainty of demand and the asymmetry of information in health care.

Arrow (1963) has suggested that the demand for health care involves a great deal of uncertainty, making health care unlike other sectors. One does not know when one is likely to become ill, for how long, and at what expense. Indeed, a major reason for insurance coverage in health care is to guard against uncertain and potentially expensive events. Unlike other types of uncertain events in the economy, such as a random destruction of property, health care insurance is subject to moral hazard. That is, when health care services are covered by insurance, more services are likely to be consumed than without coverage. In contrast, one does not ordinarily set fire to one's own home because of insurance coverage.

Pauly (1978) has suggested that the most important difference between health care and other sectors is the asymmetry of information between the providers of health care and the potential purchasers of health care. Physicians, for example, often know a great deal about how to treat an illness, but the patient may have the illness for the first time and know little about the course of treatment. There are times when even the physician is unaware of the appropriate course of treatment for the patient. One may ask, however, if other specialized occupations, such as plumbing, accounting, or law, do not have the same information asymmetries between the sellers and the potential consumers.

A number of other factors might account for differences between health care and other sectors—for example, the existence of nonprofit firms, such as many acute care hospitals, nursing homes, and home health agencies. But in other sectors of the economy, nonprofit institutions, such as schools and universities, travel clubs (such as AAA), museums, and day care centers, are dominant. Some observers might suggest that health care is different because of the extensive amount of government regulation and financing of health care. At the federal, state, and local levels, health care is extensively regulated by government. For example, health insurance firms may have to meet financial solvency standards; physicians must meet licensure requirements; and quality of care may be regulated in nursing homes. Yet other sectors in the economy are regulated in ways that are similar to government regulation in health care. Life, automobile, and other insurance is regulated; automobiles and airplanes must have certain safety equipment; real estate agents, beauticians, and many other persons need licenses to practice their occupations; and agricultural products must meet certain weight and ingredient requirements.

Government purchases approximately one-third of health care output, mostly because of the Medicare program for the elderly and the Medicaid program for the indigent. But other sectors, such as defense, in which the government buys virtually all output, may be understood by using traditional economic analysis.

Finally, the role of physicians may differentiate health care from other sectors. The physician often acts as the gatekeeper in the system; a patient cannot enter a hospital without a physician's approval. A physician's approval is also necessary for certain tests and procedures and for prescriptions of pharmaceuticals. Others play specialized roles, however, both inside and outside the health care sector. An individual does not generally bring litigation or purchase a home without an attorney, for instance, and a university student might be prohibited from enrolling in particular classes without a professor's or dean's approval.

Economics and Efficiency

Economics is concerned with an efficient allocation of resources. In the economist's jargon, efficiency from the seller's standpoint occurs when the marginal (or incremental) costs of producing and delivering the product are equal to the price received for the product.

Pure competition model

Figure 1.2 illustrates a firm under the pure competition market structure, the economist's paradigm wherein marginal cost equals price at the profit-maximizing equilibrium output. This firm may produce either a good or a service. By the definition of pure competition, this firm is also producing at least cost; hence, price not only equals marginal cost but also equals the lowest point of the average total cost

Figure 1.2 A Single Firm in the Pure Competition Model

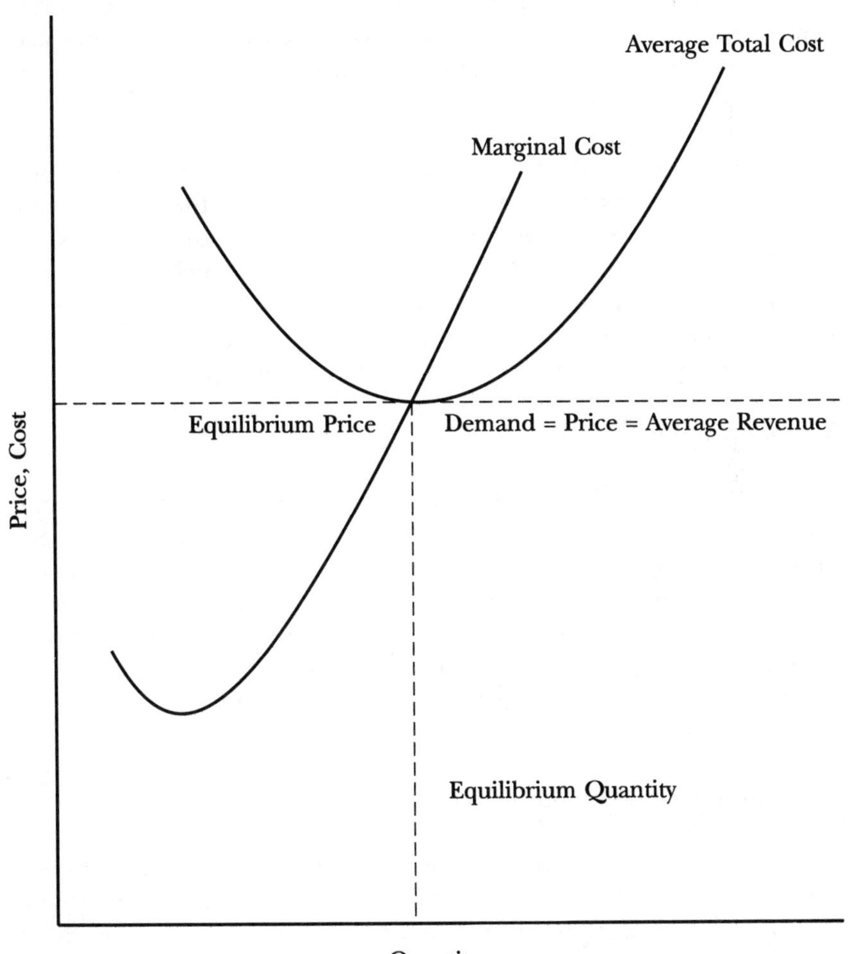

curve. Average costs are the total costs of the firm divided by the number of units produced. Moreover, supranormal profits, measured as the difference between price and average cost, must be equal to zero in the long run.

The pure competition model for an entire industry involves a number of conditions. These conditions are (1) a large number of firms, no one of which can influence price; (2) an absence of barriers to entry to new firms that might seek to enter the industry; (3) identical goods or services being sold by each of the firms in the industry; and (4) perfect information about prices, quality, and output on the part of both consumers and firms.

These conditions suggest that the demand curve, average revenue curve, or price curve is perfectly horizontal rather than downward sloping since a single firm could not raise its price without losing sales to the other firms in the industry that are selling the same good or service. The firm would also be foolish to lower its price since it can make all sales at the equilibrium price.

Although no industries meet these criteria precisely (the wheat and corn industries are generally considered to be the closest examples), the pure competition paradigm serves as a model against which all firms and industries may be measured and with which all other economic models may be compared. The three most common economic structural models, in addition to pure competition (see Figure 1.2), are monopoly, monopolistic competition, and oligopoly.

Monopoly model

Under the monopoly model, in a market in which there is a single seller, the price is not equal to but above marginal cost. This model is illustrated in Figure 1.3. Unlike pure competition, monopoly accords supranormal profits to the firm since price also exceeds average total cost. Monopolies may arise when the easy-entry assumption of pure competition is violated and the entry of rivals is barred. A single hospital in a town where regulatory barriers inhibit the entry of new entrants may be considered to be a monopoly.

Monopolistic competition model

Monopolistic competition has some of the attributes of the monopoly and pure competition models. Entry is relatively easy, but firms attempt to differentiate their products. This product differentiation may allow firms to make supranormal profits like monopolies, but since entry

Figure 1.3 A Monopoly Firm

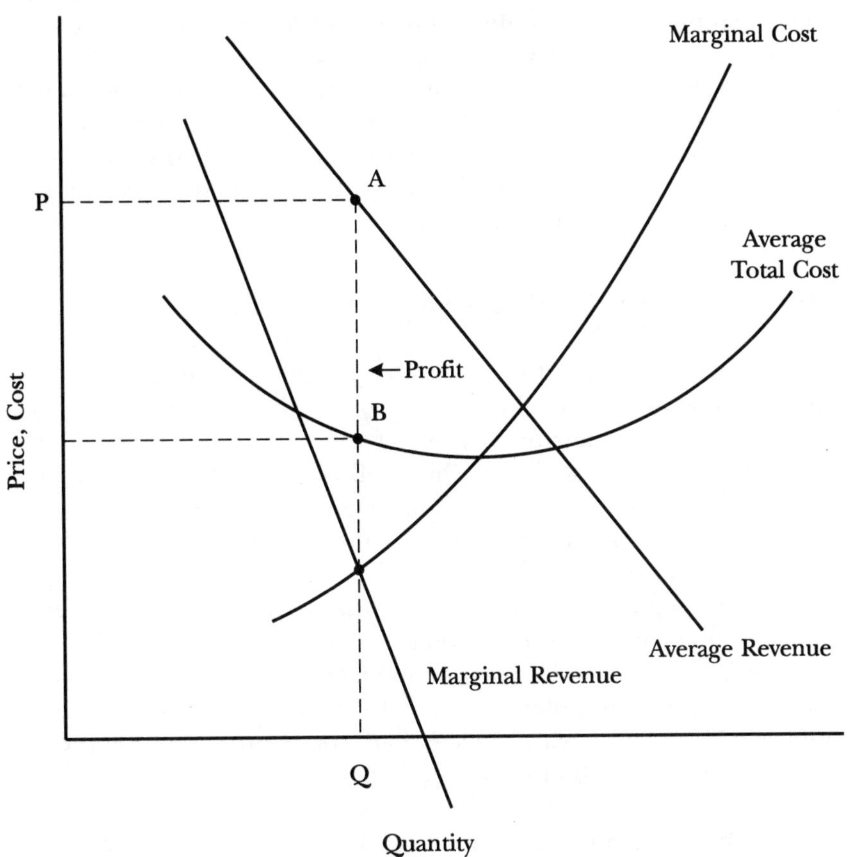

is relatively easy, firms cannot make supranormal profits in the long run. Such profits would be dissipated by potential new entrants responding to the higher short-run profits. The health insurance industry may be considered monopolistically competitive since there are more than 300 firms attempting to differentiate their products under conditions of relatively easy entry.

Oligopoly model

The oligopolistic industry is characterized by a few firms, difficult entry, and prices usually above marginal costs. The oligopolistic model may resemble the monopoly model, but substantial competition can evolve even with only a few firms in an industry. When entry is difficult, however, oligopolists may collude on price and charge prices above marginal costs. Variations on the theme do occur, though, so that some models of oligopoly depict relatively easy entry with prices reduced to the competitive level; in this case, the oligopoly model may resemble the monopolistic competition model. Firms in oligopolistic industries may sell undifferentiated products (e.g., steel) or differentiated products (e.g., automobiles). A few hospitals in a small town may be considered an oligopoly.

Efficiency in the Health Care Sector

These four market structures—pure competition, monopoly, monopolistic competition, and oligopoly—provide clues to the factors necessary to make the health care sector efficient. In industries in the real world, it is impossible to achieve all of the elements of the pure competition model. Economists, however, examine some aspects of the pure competition model more closely than others in ascertaining an industry's efficiency.

For example, economists believe that reduced barriers to entry are essential if prices are to gravitate toward marginal costs. Reduced barriers can also engender competition from existing firms since there would be a threat of potential entry if prices became too high in the industry. In addition, with reduced barriers to entry, there are incentives for sellers to produce efficiently and cater to consumer desires or risk going out of business. If the costs that firms bear in the long run are higher than the prices they charge, firms will have to exit from the industry. Even firms with a reasonably large market share or in a monopoly position will have incentives to produce as efficiently as possible since they could always realize higher profits. Similarly, increased information in the marketplace will help sellers make decisions about whether and when to enter an industry. Increased information will enable consumers to seek out the sellers whose price and quality attributes they desire.

In contrast, economists have virtually ignored the homogeneous product condition of pure competition as a requirement of an efficient industry. This is because of a realization that products that are differentiated offer expanded choices to consumers. In addition, economists give the condition of a large number of small sellers less standing as an efficiency criterion since the potential of large sellers to realize economies of scale may result in lower costs.

Sources of market imperfections

There are a number of sources of market imperfections in an industry. Information conveyed to buyers through advertising by sellers, for example, may be imperfect, misleading, or deceptive. In general, sellers have incentives to provide accurate information or risk alienating potential buyers. Nevertheless, some sellers may choose to maximize short-run profits by knowingly providing inaccurate information to consumers. If this is the case, consumers may purchase goods and services at a price that exceeds expected benefits or where initially perceived quality is greater than actual quality. The Federal Trade Commission has attempted to reduce misleading or deceptive advertising by filing suit, under Section 5 of the Federal Trade Commission Act, against firms that engage in such practices.

The presence of externalities is another source of market imperfection. Externalities are social benefits or costs that accrue not only to the buyer of the good or service but to other individuals as well. For example, the social benefit, or positive externality, of a vaccination against a communicable disease accrues not only to those who are vaccinated but to others who are now less likely to contract the disease. A social cost, or negative externality, occurs when the pollution generated by a factory affects individuals who are not buyers of the factory's product. In health care, a negative externality may occur when the consumption of alcohol destroys not only an alcoholic's own life but also the lives of his or her family.

When social benefits are involved, government has sometimes subsidized the buyer of the service to encourage greater consumption than would be the case if the buyer had to purchase the service unassisted. County health departments, for example, often provide free vaccinations. When social costs are involved, government has often taxed the product to reduce the amount of it that would be purchased. Alcoholic beverages, for example, carry substantial federal and state taxes.

Market imperfections can be caused by long-run decreasing average costs in an industry. In this case, the firm with the lowest costs may expand and achieve still lower costs. It may then be able to charge lower prices and to dominate the industry. This single firm is a natural monopoly. To retain the benefits for society of decreasing costs and economies of scale, economists have suggested that natural monopolies be regulated. Many electric and gas utilities with large power plants have been regulated for this reason.

Finally, a market imperfection or failure may occur in the production of public goods. A public good is a good or service that benefits not only a single individual but an entire community of individuals. The production of biomedical research might be an example. No single individual would pay the costs of such research since the benefits generally accrue to all of society. Often, then, biomedical research is funded by charitable donations, with some nonpecuniary recognition of the philanthropists, or by the government.

Economists have agreed that there is economic justification for some government intervention in the economy, although they have disagreed about its appropriate forms or where regulation should take place. In Chapter 7, we will examine in detail the justifications for government intervention and their applicability to the health care sector. Moreover, we will also explore government intervention that does not have as its primary goal the achievement of economic efficiency.

In some instances, government may intervene to help make an industry more competitive not because of a market imperfection but because a seller or sellers appear to monopolize an industry. For example, firms may find it profitable to collude on price or output, acquire competitors, or eliminate the competition of low-cost firms. Since 1890, antitrust laws have attempted to curtail these practices in nearly every sector of the economy. Since 1975, when the Federal Trade Commission filed suit against the American Medical Association (AMA), government has applied antitrust policy to the health care sector. The intent of antitrust policy and enforcement, which we will examine more fully in Chapter 8, is to encourage competition rather than to impose increased regulation on the economy.

Economic efficiency and equity

One form of government intervention in the economy deserves particular emphasis: the provision of subsidies in kind or in cash to individuals whom society considers to have an inadequate amount of a particular good or service. The food stamp and Aid to Families with Dependent Children (AFDC) programs are examples of such subsidies, as are certain housing programs. Although society may decide to provide subsidies for various reasons, one consideration is society's interest in promoting equity in the distribution of certain goods and services.

In the health care sector as well as in the rest of the economy, efficient allocation of resources does not guarantee equitable distribution of the goods and services produced. Differences in income levels, geographic location, and insurance coverage, for example, make it extremely unlikely that health care services will be uniformly provided to all individuals. Moreover, economists cannot even agree on a definition of what constitutes an equitable distribution of goods and services. Economists can, however, provide data and examine the trade-offs in the achievement of a more equitable distribution. Economists can also suggest some ways, including government intervention, to alter the distribution of services. In Chapter 11 these alternatives will be carefully examined.

Economic efficiency and rationing

The price system is the most efficient way to allocate goods and services in the economy. Because of the impersonal nature of the price system, a bureaucracy is not needed to decide who gets what and how much of a good or service. In the health care sector, however, society has an aversion to allocating services based on price alone. More than 65 percent of health care expenditures are paid by insurance, which insulates individuals from the effects of many health care prices. Some nonprice criteria, such as patient's health status and age in the case of heart transplants, are used as rationing devices instead. As more transplants are performed, technological advances are introduced, and new procedures become available, it is possible that nonprice rationing will assume a larger role in the health care sector. In Chapter 10, I will examine rationing in the health care sector in much more detail.

Physician Services

In Chapter 2, I will examine the market for physician services. Physicians have been called the captains of the health care team for good reason. In addition to their own relatively high incomes, physicians account for approximately 70 percent of health care expenditures by ordering tests, procedures, and pharmaceuticals; admitting patients to hospitals; and authorizing length of stay in hospitals. The aim of the next chapter will be to describe physician behavior as well as to highlight the market imperfections in this industry.

References

Arrow, K. (1963). "Uncertainty and the Welfare Economics of Medical Care," *American Economic Review* 53: 941–73.

Pauly, M. V. (1978). "Is Medical Care Different?" In *Competition in the Health Care Sector: Past, Present, and Future*, ed. W. Greenberg, 11–35. Germantown, MD: Aspen Systems Corporation.

2

The Physician Services Industry

Although physicians receive only about 20 percent of the nation's expenditures on health care, they influence the amount of hospital care and pharmaceuticals consumed and the number of medical tests performed. The total of these expenditures accounts for nearly two-thirds of health care expenses.

There were more than 550,000 physicians in the United States in 1985, 81 percent of them involved in patient care (American Medical Association 1986, 11). Although this may appear to be a large number of physicians, they are not, of course, all in competition with one another. There is almost no competition, for example, among physicians in some specialties, such as pathology and obstetrics. Table 2.1 shows physicians according to major specialty areas.

Between 1965 and 1985, the total number of physicians increased 89.2 percent from 292,088 to 552,716, while the nation's population increased only 23.1 percent (American Medical Association 1986, 19; U.S. Bureau of the Census 1990). In part, the disproportionate increase in the supply of physicians may be due to the Health Professions Educational Assistance Act of 1963. This Act authorized matching grants for the construction of medical schools, as well as loans for medical students. Moreover, in 1965, Congress authorized additional construction of medical schools and scholarships for needy students (Grupenhoff and Strickland 1972, 4–6).

There has also been a large increase in the number of professionals who may substitute for physicians in the provision of some health care services. The number of psychologists and optometrists, for example, has increased between 1977 and 1987. In 1977, there were 13,378 psychologists and 20,300 optometrists, while in 1987 there were 28,147 psychologists and 24,500 optometrists, an increase of 110 percent and 21 percent, respectively (Plon, in press; Aron 1991). Moreover, in 1986

Table 2.1 Number of Physicians, by Specialty, 1985

Specialty	*Number of Physicians*
Family practice	40,021
General practice	27,030
Anesthesiology	22,021
General surgery	38,169
Internal medicine	90,417
Obstetrics/gynecology	30,867
Orthopedic surgery	17,166
Pathology	15,456
Pediatrics	35,617
Psychiatry	32,255
All other specialties	203,697
Total number of physicians	552,716

Source: American Medical Association (1986). *Physician Characteristics and Distribution in the U.S., 1986,* Chicago: The Association, 19.

there were 15,000 nurse practitioners, 16,000 physician assistants, and 2,000 certified nurse-midwives practicing in the United States (U.S. Congress 1986). This rapid increase in the number of physicians and other medical professionals will, like any increase in the supply of labor, affect the price and quantity of services delivered. The projected effect would be to shift the supply curve of physician manpower to the right, which would, for any given service, decrease the price and increase the quantity supplied. As shown below, there is some debate about the actual extent and direction of changes in price due to shifts in the supply curve.

The number of physicians in the United States has not always increased this rapidly. Prior to 1965, it appears that the physicians' political lobby exerted downward pressure on the supply of medical manpower. From the early part of the twentieth century until the mid-1960s, the American Medical Association attempted to limit the supply of physicians through its licensing of medical schools. In 1906 the Council on Medical Education of the American Medical Association approved training in only 82 of the 160 medical schools existing at that time (Kessel 1958, 27). By 1944, the American Medical Association had reduced the number of certified medical schools to 69 (Kessel 1958, 28).

Limiting entry of new professionals and firms into a market shifts the supply curve backward to the left and allows professionals and firms already in the market to increase their income by charging fees above the competitive level. Friedman and Kuznets (1945, 67–68, 74) reported that between 1929 and 1934 income for physicians was four times higher than for the average worker. Friedman and Kuznets attributed this large relative difference, even after taking into account the educational costs and delayed employment of physicians, to the barriers to entry posed by the licensing structures of the American Medical Association. More recently, Sloan and Feldman (1978, 46) reported that physicians earn higher incomes over their lifetime than other professionals, even when a correction is made for longer hours and education.

Many other professions have also relied on licensing to limit the number of entrants. In the late nineteenth century, plumbers, barbers, blacksmiths, pharmacists, and embalmers, among other groups, were licensed by the state legislatures. Modern-day professional groups and industries have attempted to limit entry via licensing requirements and other entry barriers. By making it difficult to pass the dental licensure examinations, for example, various states, at the behest of the state dental associations, have made it nearly impossible for out-of-state dentists to practice in their states (Shepard 1978).

How Do Physicians Compete?

Firms usually compete on a number of dimensions—price, quality, convenience, durability, and design. Firms may also compete on products that contain new technology or innovation.

Physicians compete on a number of different levels. First, physicians compete for patients who are able to pay for services and do not have health insurance, or whose insurance requires them to pay a deductible or copayment when utilizing physician services. These patients, in general, may choose any physician they wish.

Second, since more than 60 percent of expenditures on physician services are paid by third-party insurers, making patients somewhat, but not entirely, indifferent to price, most physicians elect to compete primarily on a nonprice basis. Competition may be based on location, colleagues' referrals, or reputation. New, less-established physicians have even begun to advertise their services (Rizzo and Zeckhauser 1990). One rarely observes surgical specialists, whose services are heavily covered by insurance, engaging in price competition.

Third, physicians may compete for affiliation with a preferred provider organization (PPO) that offers a preferred group of physicians as part of its benefit package. To be selected as part of a preferred group of physicians, a physician may have to offer reduced fees to the organization and agree to utilization reviews. In addition, a physician may have to meet certain standards of quality established by the organization.

Pricing Strategies of Physicians

Kessel (1958) has suggested that most physicians engage in price discrimination. They charge higher fees to patients with higher incomes and lower fees to patients with lower incomes. In addition, physicians may charge higher fees to those with health insurance and lower fees to those without insurance. Put another way, physicians set their prices based on elasticity of demand. Higher-income individuals or those with health insurance usually have less elastic demands (the relative change in quantity demanded will be small compared to the relative change in price), while lower-income individuals or those with little insurance have more elastic demands (the relative change in quantity demanded will be large compared to the relative change in price). In the price discrimination model the income a physician earns exceeds even a monopoly return, because individuals will buy the service at above as well as below the monopoly price.

Price discrimination is not peculiar to the physician services industry. A Broadway theatre, for example, may charge higher prices for Saturday-evening performances, for which demand is less elastic, than for Saturday-matinee performances, for which demand is more elastic. Airlines also use price discrimination when they set higher prices for last-minute business travel, for which demand is least elastic, and lower prices for off-season vacation trips, for which demand is most elastic. To use price discrimination, physicians or firms must have some monopolistic power, such that other firms would not readily be able to charge lower prices and take away customers when prices are set at relatively high levels by the price discriminating firm. Price discrimination, then, can be a symptom of at least some monopoly power. Many believe that most of this monopoly power began with the original American Medical Association restrictions on entry.

In a competitive marketplace, an increase in the supply of a good or service will result in a decline in price, all other factors held equal. Further, at the lower price a greater quantity of the good or service will be sold. Evans (1974) has suggested, however, that physicians can set their own prices and earn a target income without regard to changes in the demand for and the supply of physician services.

First, according to Evans, the asymmetry of information between the physician and the patient is such that the physician generally knows the prices of a great variety of office visits and procedures, but the patient generally knows very little about relative prices. Thus, patient ignorance of prices enables the physician to charge a price higher than would be possible under competitive conditions. Second, the target income hypothesis suggests that each physician has at least some monopoly power to set his or her own fees. This may be especially true when only a few specialists practice in a particular area and, therefore, may be able to charge a higher fee because of limited competition. Third, the extent of insurance for physician services suggests that patients will be somewhat indifferent to the prices charged and that to this degree physicians can set their own fees.

Pauly and Satterthwaite (1981) examined the role of consumer information and physician fees. They examined primary care physicians only since insurance coverage is comparatively modest for this segment of the physician population. The authors suggested that fees might be higher, not lower, in an area with an increased number of physicians because the greater the number of physicians in a particular area, the more difficult it is for patients to compare physician fees. The comparison is difficult, according to the authors, because most information on physician fees is shared by word of mouth among patients, which makes fees more difficult to compare and search costs greater as the number of physicians increases.

In contrast to this view of the physician services market, a more traditional view suggests that the price for physician services is no higher and, in fact, may be lower when there are a greater number of physicians. In areas with an abundance of physicians, waiting times may be shorter and visits longer, thereby increasing the quality of visits and reducing the real price. Quality may also be measured by the types of specialists who practice in high-density areas. Because of the nature of specialty practice, the specialist may deliver a more valuable service, which can engender a higher price (Feldman and Sloan 1988). In addition, it is possible that higher fees in an area may attract a greater number of physicians, reversing the causality from physicians generating higher fees to higher fees inducing more physicians to practice in the area. Further, one may ask why, if physicians have the ability to set prices so as to achieve a particular target income, they have not attempted to set a price that is even higher and might bring them even more income.

Creating Their Own Demand?

When General Motors, with a great deal of advertising, offers its new line of automobiles in the fall, is the company creating its own demand if people buy the cars? Are fashion designers creating their own demand when they introduce new fall and spring lines of clothes? Is McDonald's creating its own demand when it opens a new restaurant? Perhaps, instead, these firms are meeting a demand that is already present and, by extensive advertising or a more convenient location, are informing individuals of a product's existence or reducing the traveling time in buying the product. These examples suggest that "demand creation" can be a complex phenomenon and that a simple increase in the number of goods or services provided does not necessarily mean that demand has been created.

The physician is both the agent for the patient and the provider of services. Demand for physician services may increase when it becomes less costly to visit physicians. With an increase in the supply of physicians, for example, transportation costs may be reduced for physician office visits. On the other hand, consumption of physician services may rise if, given the patient's lack of knowledge of physician procedures, the physician elects to perform more procedures than the patient would purchase with perfect knowledge of appropriate procedures. However, even with asymmetry of information, there are some constraints on a physician's ability to create demand.

First, in not all visits is there an asymmetry of information. For many pediatric visits, for example, parents have at least some knowledge of the range of tests that might be involved in a well-baby examination. Second, physicians have an incentive to keep existing patients and may, like any firm, exercise care about increasing clients' expenditures. Third, for some examinations and procedures, there are costs of discomfort and inconvenience to the patient, which increase the overall costs of visiting a physician and thereby limit demand.

The support offered for the hypothesis that physicians can create their own demand tends not to be whether a particular physician can, with impunity, order or perform additional services for a given patient, but rather whether an increased number of physicians (usually expressed in terms of an increased physician-to-population ratio) results in more services delivered per physician than the number of services delivered per physician in an area with fewer physicians.

When there is a greater supply of physicians, one would expect an increase in the number of services delivered, just as one would expect an increase in the supply of any commodity to result in a greater quantity of the commodity supplied. An increase in the supply of a commodity, all other factors held constant, would mean a reduction in the price of the commodity and hence an increase in the number of services delivered or purchased. Therefore, if the number of services increases with an increase in physician supply, it may simply be because of a reduction in the price of the services.

Moreover, although it has been shown that an increase in the number of surgeries in an area is associated with a higher physician-to-population ratio, this does not prove that physicians can increase the number of these surgeries. There may be, for example, an in-migration of patients into areas with a large number of surgeons or prestigious hospitals such as from the surrounding cities of New Jersey and Connecticut into New York City or from the surrounding cities of New England into Boston.

Recent geographic changes in the health care marketplace have cast additional doubt on physicians' ability to create their own demand. A study by RAND Corporation economists shows, for example, that an increasing number of physicians are establishing practices in the rural areas of the United States as opposed to the cities and suburbs. Currently, very few towns of populations greater than 2,500 do not have at least some physicians (Williams, Schwartz, Newhouse, and Bennett 1983). Traditionally, physicians have located their offices in the major cities near the more prestigious hospitals. Although it is possible that there may be noneconomic reasons why individuals have begun practices in the rural areas, the difficulty that physicians face in earning high incomes in the large cities—where there is intense competition—may be an important factor in that movement.

Wennberg and Gittelsohn (1973) found substantial geographic variation in the number of surgeries physicians performed for the same diagnosis even within the same state. This may not necessarily mean, however, that physicians can create their own demand. Rather, without further evidence, the variation may suggest the difficulties of making informed judgments in medicine and the uncertainty surrounding those judgments. Variations in practice patterns may also be influenced by financial considerations such as reimbursement practices of third-party payers, income of individuals receiving treatment, and for some procedures, physician ownership of freestanding diagnostic or imaging centers. The Agency for Health Care Policy and Research within the U.S. Public Health Service, created in 1989, is charged with the mandate to help assess the effectiveness of medical interventions and outcomes (Salive, Mayfield, and Weissman 1990). By disseminating the results of effectiveness studies, it is hoped that new medical treatments and technology will not only be used in a cost-effective manner but also that functional outcomes of treatment will be improved.

When a Third-Party Payer is Purchaser

The ability of physicians to create their own demand or to set their own prices depends heavily on the assumption that patients lack information. If patients had as much information as physicians on the efficacy of individual procedures, procedures would not be performed when benefits to the patient approached zero. If individuals knew the fees that physicians charged, a dispersion of fees within a given area would reflect only differences in the quality of care the physicians provided. Quality remaining constant, individuals would avoid the higher-priced physicians, which would put downward pressure on the higher fees until they eventually equaled the fees of other physicians (Stigler 1961).

Insurance covers approximately 60 percent of physician services. The insurer, public or private, may well be able to supply some of the information that the individual patient does not have. Unlike the patient, the insurer has reviewed many similar cases. With this information, the insurer is in a position to question nonemergency procedures and visits as well as physician fees. Many utilization review and managed care techniques by insurers are efforts in this direction. The insurer can help close the window of asymmetric information. The ultimate form of control against any demand creation is the health maintenance organization (HMO), which has built-in financial incentives to curtail excessive utilization. Insurers also have strong bargaining power in many geographic areas and may be able to limit excessive utilization by forming preferred provider organizations.

Most of the data used in empirical tests of physicians' ability to create demand or to set fees were gathered prior to the extensive utilization review and cost-containment efforts on the part of insurers in the 1980s. Because of cost containment by insurers, it is not clear that future studies will be able to show correlations between physician supply and physician fees or between physician supply and services performed. If anything, the growing importance of the active third-party payer has made it more difficult for physicians to create their own demand.

There is no reason to believe that physicians create their own demand at a greater rate than any other professional group. Phrases such as "physician surplus" and "physician glut" appear to be too glib in describing the market for physician services. Empirical and theoretical evidence has yet to support strongly and unequivocally the notion that physicians can induce their own demand without limit. Nevertheless, the presence of third-party insurance reduces the net price of care to patients, which will increase the number of services delivered regardless of whether physicians can induce their own demand. Utilization review has distinct limitations in curtailing the number of services delivered since many services may be justified as having benefits greater than the net price paid by patients (see Chapter 10).

Additional Aspects of Physician Competition

There are at least four additional ways that physicians have elected to compete in the medical marketplace: by creating individual practice associations (IPAs), by influencing the reimbursement practices of Blue Shield, by attempting to reduce the competition from nonphysicians, and by advertising physician services.

Creating individual practice associations

Physicians may react to competition from alternative delivery systems or health maintenance organizations in a number of ways. For example, physicians have begun their own IPAs. Typically, these IPAs are based on a physician organization that in turn contracts with individual physicians. There is some utilization review, although physicians continue to practice in a fee-for-service manner. In this way, the IPA expects to achieve lower costs than if each of its member physicians were to practice individually.

Influencing Blue Shield reimbursement practices

Many Blue Shield plans were begun by physicians in the 1930s to guarantee payment of physician services and to reduce the cost-containment pressures of other third-party insurers and prepaid plans. Physicians have continued to participate on the boards of Blue Shield plans. In many states, physicians have made up the majority of the board of the directors of the plan; in other states, a physician has been the chairperson of the board. In still other states, physicians do not constitute the majority of the board of directors but may nominate a large proportion of the board. In every Blue Shield plan in the United States, there has been at least one physician on the board of directors. A study by the U.S. Federal Trade Commission (1979) has suggested that physicians' influence on the boards of Blue Shield plans has led to higher fees than would have been the case without physicians on the boards. Alternative delivery systems, however, have reduced Blue Shield's market share and thus its ability to pay higher fees to physicians.

Reducing competition from nonphysicians

There has been substantial physician resistance to hospital staff privileges for psychologists, podiatrists, and other nonphysician health professionals (see Chapter 8). Further, the Federal Trade Commission has brought a number of cases challenging physicians' conduct in attempting to curb the practice of nonphysicians. One such case resulted in a consent decree with State Volunteer Mutual Insurance Company, a physician-owned malpractice insurance firm that denied insurance to physicians who supervised self-employed nurse-midwives. The FTC complaint alleged that competition between physicians and nurse-midwives would be restricted if nurse-midwives could not practice independently (see Chapter 8). Restricting the competition of nonphysicians, to the extent that their services could not be substituted for those of physicians, would increase the demand for physician services.

Advertising physician services

In 1975, the Federal Trade Commission brought suit against the American Medical Association for restricting physician advertising. The case eventually reached the Supreme Court, which ruled on it in 1982, *American Medical Association v. Federal Trade Commission,* 455 US 676 (1982). In an equally divided opinion, the Supreme Court affirmed a lower court's ruling, which upheld a decision against the American Medical Association for violating Section 5 of the Federal Trade Commission Act. Since 1982, therefore, physicians have been free to advertise.

Advertising, or product differentiation, may take various forms. Advertising may be placed in print or broadcast media. It may be used to build up a trademark or brand name. It may focus on the quality or price of a good or service, or on new technological breakthroughs. Many physicians advertise their availability, location, and specialties. Hospitals may advertise the availability of physicians on their staff, in the expectation that if individuals use their physicians, the physicians, in turn, will refer patients to their hospitals.

Because of the presence of insurance, it is relatively unimportant for physicians to advertise the price of their services. This is especially true for services heavily covered by insurance, such as radiologic or surgical services. Physicians have also not advertised explicit measures of their performance, such as the proficiency of their surgery. This is consistent with the behavior of other professional groups, such as attorneys and accountants, who also do not advertise the quality of their work. It is unclear why these professionals do not advertise quality, unless word of mouth or the reputation of the firm with which they are affiliated is a more efficient method of disseminating this information.

Preferred provider organizations may also engage in physician advertising. In return for physicians' acceptance of reduced fees and utilization review, preferred provider organizations generally advertise the availability of their member physicians.

Advertising in the physician services industry may distribute patients to different physicians with approximately the same overall number of office visits or may increase the total demand for physician services. For services with an inelastic demand, such as emergency medicine, the total number of visits will remain the same. For services with a more elastic demand, such as plastic surgery, the total number of physician visits may increase.

The Performance of Physicians

This chapter has attempted to show that the market performance of the physician services industry can respond to the forces of supply and demand. When supply was restricted by the American Medical Association, physician income increased. When demand increased because of the institution of Medicare and Medicaid in 1965, physician income also increased. When the supply of physicians and nonphysician professionals began to increase in the mid-1970s, physicians' net incomes (adjusted for inflation) began to stabilize (Gonzalez 1986).

The rate of increase in malpractice premiums and the number of malpractice suits might appear to be a helpful guide to physician performance. These variables, however, depend very heavily on changes in the types of procedures performed as well as changes in the malpractice laws of the various states.

In addition to the performance of the physician services industry as a whole, one might also be concerned with the performance of individual physicians. To evaluate a surgeon, for example, a prospective patient might want to know the surgeon's mortality rates adjusted by patient mix, hospital personnel with whom the surgeon worked, type of hospital equipment, and other factors. To date, there has been no attempt to evaluate physicians on these objective criteria, although there does not appear to be any relationship between mortality rates and the number of surgeries performed by individual surgeons (Kelly and Hellinger, 1986). The amount of malpractice litigation against individual physicians also does not appear to be a good indicator of performance. For example, Sloan et al. (1989) found no significant relationship between physician quality and malpractice litigation.

Malpractice and physicians

Only $5 billion was spent on medical malpractice premiums by all medical providers in 1988, or less than 1 per cent of health care expenditures (U.S. Congress 1991, 22–23). Malpractice premiums paid by physicians may not describe completely the potential for malpractice to alter physician supply as well as to increase the costs of health care. Increasing premiums in medical specialties, such as obstetrics/gynecology, may reduce the supply and hours worked of these physicians. Premiums paid by physicians may also increase the price of physician services depending on the elasticity of demand. The fear of malpractice litigation by physicians may also encourage a greater number of tests, procedures, and physician office visits. It is difficult to estimate, however, the extent of any additional costs. Tests, procedures, and physician office visits in which there is virtually no benefit may be curtailed by managed-care plans. However, there are also tests and procedures that may increase health care costs but improve quality as well (U.S. Congress 1991, 22–23).

There are clearly no natural monopolies or economies of scale in the physician services industry. The licensing of physicians can always create a barrier to entry into physician services. Licensing does convey some information to the patient that the physician has demonstrated some minimal level of expertise. Yet the testing of physician competence might be made at periodic intervals rather than simply at graduation from medical school.

There are imperfections in information between physician and patient. All physicians, whether in tight or abundant supply, may be able to perform more services at higher prices than a fully informed patient would demand. The increase in physician advertising should help provide information to patients on at least the location of physician offices and the type of service the physician performs. Moreover, third-party payers and employers are beginning to supply their enrollees with information on physician fees. Even state governments are beginning to provide information on physician fees.

At the federal level, the development of the National Practitioners Data Bank may make it more difficult for suboptimal physicians to practice medicine. Physicians whose medical licenses or hospital privileges have been suspended for 30 days or more, or who have had malpractice settlements, will be listed in a National Practitioners Data Bank. Although the public will not be able to see the data, information will be made available to hospital peer review boards and state licensing boards. In this way, the hospital may act as agent for the patient in refusing to grant staff privileges to physicians it finds unacceptable.

Potential imperfections in physician services that stem from the presence of insurance can best be covered in Chapter 4 on the private insurance sector. For example, the fact that physicians may perform too many services or that the fees for some services are higher than marginal costs might reflect the nature of insurance. Aside from the presence of insurance, however, it is not surprising that the primary care physician services market has been termed a monopolistically competitive market (McCarthy 1985). For other physician services such as orthopedic surgery, radiology, and obstetrics/gynecology, which are heavily covered by insurance, physician incomes appear to be above the competitive equilibrium level. Orthopedic surgeons, radiologists, and obstetricians made net incomes of $219,120, $185,000, and $157,930, respectively, in 1988 (Owens 1989).

References

American Medical Association (1986). *Physician Characteristics and Distribution in the U.S.,1986.* Chicago: The Association.

Aron, F. (1991). Personal Communication. Manager, Information and Data, American Optometric Association, St. Louis.

Evans, R. G. (1974). "Supplier-Induced Demand: Some Empirical Evidence and Implications." In *The Economics of Health and Medical Care,* ed. M. Perlman, 162–73. New York: John Wiley & Sons, Inc.

Feldman, R., and Sloan, F. A. (1988). "Competition Among Physicians, Revisited." In *Competition in the Health Care Sector: Ten Years Later,* ed. W. Greenberg, 17–39. Durham, NC: Duke University Press.

Friedman, M., and Kuznets, S. (1945). *Income from Independent Professional Practice.* New York: National Bureau of Economic Research.

Gonzalez, M. L. (1986). "Physician Income Trends, 1975–85." In *Socioeconomic Characteristics of Medical Practice, 1986,* ed. M. L. Gonzalez and D. W. Emmons, 17–21. Chicago: American Medical Association.

Grupenhoff, J., and Strickland, S., eds. (1972). *Federal Laws: Health/Environment Manpower.* Washington, DC: Washington Science and Health Communications Group.

Kelly, J. V., and Hellinger, F. J. (1986). "Physician and Hospital Factors Associated with Mortality of Surgical Patients," *Medical Care* 24: 785–800.

Kessel, R. A. (1958). "Price Discrimination in Medicine," *Journal of Law and Economics* 1: 20–53.

McCarthy, T. R. (1985). "The Competitive Nature of the Primary-Care Physician Services Market," *Journal of Health Economics* 4: 93–117.

Owens, A. (1989). "Earnings: Are You One of Those Losing Ground?" *Medical Economics* 66: 131–150.

Pauly, M. V., and Satterthwaite, M. A. (1981). "The Pricing of Primary Care Physicians' Services: A Test of the Role of Consumer Information," *The Bell Journal of Economics* 12: 488–506.

Plon, G. M. (in press). "Psychologists Wanted: Employment Trends Over the Last Decade." In *Managing Your Psychological Career*, ed. R. Kilburg. Washington, DC: American Psychological Association.

Rizzo, J. A., and Zeckhauser, R. J. (1990). "Advertising and Entry: The Case of Physician Services," *Journal of Political Economy* 98: 476–500.

Salive, M. E., Mayfield, J. A., and Weissman, N. W. (1990). "Patient Outcomes Research Teams and the Agency for Health Care Policy and Research," *Health Services Research* 25: 697–708.

Shepard, L. (1978). "Licensing Restrictions and the Cost of Dental Care," *Journal of Law and Economics* 21: 187–201.

Sloan, F. A., and Feldman, R. (1978). "Competition Among Physicians." In *Competition in the Health Care Sector: Past, Present, and Future*, ed. W. Greenberg, 45–102. Germantown, MD.: Aspen Systems Corporation.

Sloan, F. A. et al. (1989). "Medical Malpractice Experience of Physicians," *Journal of the American Medical Association* 262: 3291–97.

Stigler, G. J. (1961). "The Economics of Information," *Journal of Political Economy* 69: 213–25.

U.S. Bureau of the Census (1990). *Statistical Abstract of the United States, 1990*, 110th Edition, p. 7. Washington, DC: U.S. Government Printing Office.

U.S. Congress, Congressional Budget Office (1991). *Rising Health Care Costs: Causes, Implications, and Strategies.* Washington, DC: U.S. Government Printing Office.

U.S. Congress, Office of Technology Assessment (1986). *Nurse Practitioners, Physician Assistants, and Certified Nurse-Midwives: A Policy Analysis* (Health Technology Case Study 37), OTA-HCS-37. Washington, DC: U.S. Government Printing Office.

U.S. Federal Trade Commission (1979). *Medical Participation in Control of Blue Shield and Certain Other Open-Panel Medical Prepayment Plans* (Staff Report to the Federal Trade Commission and Proposal Trade Regulation Rule). Washington, DC: U.S. Government Printing Office.

Wennberg, J. E., and Gittelsohn, A. (1973). "Small Area Variations in Health Care Delivery," *Science* 182: 1102–08.

Williams, A., Schwartz, W. B., Newhouse, J. P., and Bennett, B. W. (1983). "How Many Miles to the Doctor?" *New England Journal of Medicine* 309: 958–63.

3

The Hospital Industry

The people of the United States spent $212 billion dollars on hospital care in 1988 (Health Care Financing Administration 1990). Hospital care is the largest component in the health care sector, accounting for approximately 40 percent of health care expenditures. Hospital care also accounted for approximately 4 percent of the nation's $4.9 trillion gross national product in 1988.

Expenditures for hospital care have, furthermore, been growing quite rapidly. In 1966, at the beginning of the Medicare and Medicaid programs, hospital expenditures were $15.4 billion, or 2 percent of the gross national product of $747 billion (U.S. Bureau of the Census 1968). Thus, between 1966 and 1988, hospital expenditures increased fourteenfold compared to a sevenfold increase in the gross national product over the same period.

From the perspective of both the supply of hospital services and the demand for hospital services, the structure and behavior of the hospital industry have been continually changing over the past two decades. From the supply perspective, the number of nonfederal, short-term, general and special hospitals declined from 5,859 hospitals to 5,659 hospitals between 1970 and 1987 (U.S. Bureau of the Census 1990). In 1970, 10 percent of hospitals belonged to a multihospital system, while in 1986 nearly 44 percent of hospitals were members of a multihospital system (American Hospital Association 1987). For-profit hospitals constituted 13.1 percent of the hospital industry in 1970, while in 1986 for-profit hospitals made up 14.6 percent of the industry (American Hospital Association 1987; Institute of Medicine 1986a).

There have been substantial changes in the demand for hospital services. Third-party payers such as Medicare, Medicaid, Blue Cross and Blue Shield, and the commercial insurers have become much more active in attempting to control hospital costs. Some of the more common changes in hospital payment include restrictions on payments for certain procedures, use of preferred low-cost hospitals, and employment of managed care systems.

In this chapter, I will first examine the supply of hospital services. Second, I will review briefly the demand for hospital services, concentrating on the cost-containment activities of the third-party payers. Finally, I will analyze the effects of information about the quality of care in hospitals on quality, costs, and access in this industry.

The Supply of Hospital Services

In addition to short-term acute care hospitals, the hospital industry includes hospitals for psychiatric care, for tuberculosis and respiratory ailments, and for long-term general ailments. Most hospitals are nonprofit. Some observers, such as Relman (1980) have suggested that the incentives of nonprofit hospitals differ from the traditional profit-maximization incentives of for-profit hospitals in such areas as access, quality of care, teaching, and research. Most of the economic research, however, suggests that nonprofit hospitals and for-profit hospitals perform in a similar manner. In terms of access, for example, nonprofits and for-profits have a comparable record on the amount of uncompensated care they are willing to provide to low-income patients. It appears, rather, that the major difference in the accessibility of hospitals to indigent patients is between both the for-profit and nonprofit hospitals on one hand and the public hospitals on the other. Many studies have suggested that the public hospitals have a much higher proportion of indigent patients (Sloan and Vraciu 1983; Pattison and Katz 1983; Shortell 1986; Townsend 1986).

The data also suggest that the quality of care rendered in a for-profit hospital is comparable to that of a nonprofit hospital. An examination of postoperative mortality rates or readmission rates indicates no difference between nonprofit or for-profit hospitals, although these data might not describe the entire spectrum of quality of care or adjust for severity of illness (Gaumer 1986). It appears, however, that nonprofit hospitals have traditionally performed a greater amount of teaching and research than for-profit hospitals (Institute of Medicine 1986b).

Although there are a large number of hospitals, they do not all compete in the same geographic market. The theoretical market in which a hospital competes is a function of the hospital's ability to raise prices or to reduce quality without a large relative shift of patients away from that hospital to alternative hospitals. Since third-party insurance pays for more than 90 percent of hospital services, changes in price become relatively unimportant in the determination of geographic areas in which hospitals compete. After-the-fact examinations of where patients, in fact, go for hospital care are, therefore, the primary means used to determine hospital markets. The market area for a hospital's services may also depend on where physicians have staff privileges; the type of hospital (teaching or research); the distances among hospitals; and, finally, any barriers to entry in the hospital market such as certificate-of-need regulations (Morrisey, Sloan, and Valvona 1988).

State certificate-of-need laws, mandated by the National Health Planning and Resources Development Act of 1974, required that the appropriate state agency review and approve any changes in hospital bed capacity and major equipment purchases above particular dollar levels (Salkever and Bice 1976). These regulations put the burden of proof on potential hospital entrants to demonstrate the necessity of their entry into the market. With excess capacity in the industry increasing, there is less likelihood of hospital entry. Thus, certificate-of-need laws now have less influence as a barrier to entry.

Both for-profit and nonprofit hospitals have increased their membership in multihospital systems. Multihospital systems may attempt to achieve economies of scale or lower average total costs in the operations of a hospital. Multihospital systems may offer improved access to capital because of a greater asset, revenue, and equity base. Ermann and Gabel (1984) point out, however, that despite economies of scale and improved access to capital, multihospital systems may increase hospital costs because of a greater number of ancillary services delivered, higher markups, and increased capital costs. As third-party payers become more prudent in the purchase of hospital care, one would expect these higher costs to be reduced.

Hospitals have traditionally competed by accumulating the newest and latest technology in order to attract admissions by physicians (Salkever 1978). Competition among hospitals was formerly on a nonprice basis since third-party payers reimbursed hospitals for whatever prices hospitals charged and for whatever services they performed. Competition among hospitals, therefore, resulted in increased, not decreased, costs. Contrary to economic theory, the greater the number of hospitals competing in a market, the higher hospital costs might be. In this environment, where third-party payers paid on the basis of charges and costs, there were no incentives for efficient behavior among hospitals. Hospital costs continued to rise at a double-digit rate throughout the 1970s and early 1980s.

The Demand for Hospital Services

Increasing costs in hospital care precipitated changes in the demand for hospital services (Fanara and Greenberg 1985). Beginning in the 1970s and gaining momentum in the 1980s, third-party payers, both public and private, became active rather than passive payers of hospital bills.

In the public sector, most of the cost-containment efforts were regulatory. Nine states, for example, had enacted rate-setting programs by the mid-1970s. These programs ranged from total budget regulation to regulation of hospital rates. Central to these regulatory programs was the attempt to slow the rise of health care costs. It has been suggested that these programs were adopted because the rising costs of health care impinged on other needed services, such as highway construction and public education (Fanara and Greenberg 1985).

Since state regulatory payment mechanisms have usually included reimbursement for hospitals' bad debts, a secondary aim of regulation in states like Maryland and New York may have been to enable hospitals to accept indigent patients more readily (Bazzolli 1986). A third reason for rate setting by the states may have been political pressure by the hospitals themselves. In states such as Maryland, one of the objectives of the regulation was to prevent Blue Cross from achieving a preferential discount on hospital charges (Fanara and Greenberg 1985).

In other industries, firms have exerted political pressure to achieve their economic objectives. For example, in the airline industry, prior to the mid-1970s, individual firms exerted political pressure to limit entry into the industry. Many industries have lobbied extensively for protective tariffs to limit competition by foreign providers of similar goods and services (Stigler 1971).

Finally, the federal government enacted its diagnosis-related group (DRG) program in October 1983 in order to contain costs. Under this reimbursement system, hospitals are paid a fixed amount for each of 490 diagnostic-related groups for Medicare patients, regardless of the particular patient's length of stay or costs incurred. Exemptions, exceptions, or adjustments are made for hospitals that are the sole community providers; hospitals that care for a disproportionate share of low-income and Medicare patients; hospitals that are regional referral centers; hospitals that provide a large amount of cancer treatment and research; hospitals in Alaska and Hawaii; and alcohol- and drug-treatment hospitals (Prospective Payment Assessment Commission 1985, 9).

In addition to regulatory mechanisms, the state of California has instituted a competitive bidding system to reduce costs for its Medicaid (Medi-Cal) program (Johns, Anderson, and Derzon 1985). Under this system, the state requests bids from nearly all of the hospitals in the state, with the intent of doing business with hospitals that have lower costs and that are within accessible geographic areas. The state specifies a minimum range of services, and in fiscal year 1982–1983, the first year of contract negotiations, 245 of the 365 hospitals invited to negotiate were selected as Medi-Cal contract hospitals (Johns, Anderson, and Derzon 1985, 338).

The state of Arizona also began a competitive bidding system (the Arizona Health Care Cost Containment System) in 1982 to provide inpatient and other acute medical services for its indigent population. In the system's initial year, 17 of 20 organizations that submitted bids were awarded contracts (McCombs and Christianson 1987, 708). Thus far, there have been no extensive studies on the potential savings from the competitive bidding systems, but an estimate from the State Department of Health Services in California estimates savings of $184 million for fiscal year 1983–1984 (Johns 1987).

In the private sector, insurers have used a variety of methods to contain costs: for example, DRG reimbursement; competitive bidding; and alternative payment mechanisms such as preferred provider organizations. Blue Cross and Blue Shield of Arizona implemented a DRG payment system for hospitals in 1983. Blue Cross and Blue Shield of Northern Ohio has used a selective contracting approach that awards contracts only to those hospitals that have the lowest cost per case, adjusted for differences in types of cases treated. At least 50 Blue Cross and Blue Shield plans offer one or more forms of utilization review. Blue Cross and Blue Shield of Maryland formed a PPO, SelectCare, to provide an alternative to its traditional fee-for-service plans. Hospitals and physicians who agreed to become members of SelectCare were asked to reduce their rates. In return, SelectCare published the names of participating providers. Individuals who chose their physicians from the PPO did not have to pay a copayment to the provider (Greenberg 1986).

In each of these cost-containment efforts in the public and private sectors, reimbursement is based upon the price of hospital care rather than on the price and quality of hospital care. When purchasing other goods and services, consumers take both price and quality into account. Some individuals may value price more highly than quality, while others may place a higher premium on quality. Of the many goods and services purchased in the economy, one would expect hospital care to be a service whose quality is especially important to the consumer.

The Supply of Information on Quality of Care

Not only are most third-party purchases based solely on costs, but there is, in fact, not much information available on the quality of care. Thus, it is difficult for consumers, patients, and third-party payers to take quality into consideration in the purchase of hospital services.

The state of Pennsylvania, however, has begun an explicit policy to make available data on mortality rates, infections, medical complications, and readmissions to hospitals. The data are also expected to be adjusted for severity of illness (Gaul 1986). In addition, the Health Care Financing Administration (HCFA) of the Department of Health and Human Services released unadjusted Medicare mortality rates for hospitals in general as well as for 16 categories of disease within the hospital (Pear 1987). Beyond these data, however, there has been very little information on the quality of hospital care. What, then, may account for the lack of information on the quality of hospital care?

There appears to be no overt hospital association prohibition against hospitals' advertising; rather, the American Hospital Association has recommended strict guidelines, which appear to discourage aggressive marketing. The guidelines suggest that "self-aggrandizement of one hospital at the expense of another may be counterproductive, and, if inaccurate, could lead to charges of libel and claims for damages." The guidelines suggest that "quality comparisons, either direct or by implication, between one hospital's services, facilities, or employees, and those of another hospital, may be counterproductive, libelous, or difficult to present in a firm and objective manner" (American Hospital Association 1977).

Thus, while hospitals have begun to advertise, they have made only superficial comparisons of quality. Most advertising has focused on the friendliness of the staff, the quality of the food, and the convenience of the location. There are some exceptions, however. For example, the Washington Hospital Center in Washington, D.C., advertised that it performed 1,371 open-heart operations in one year, "accounting for nearly one-half of all open-heart procedures in the Washington, D.C., area" (*Washington Post* 1984).

Hospital management may also believe that overt advertising to patients is not the most efficacious way to disseminate information. Hospitals may compete instead for the allegiance of physicians, since physicians admit individuals to hospitals. Hospitals have competed, in part, by acquiring new technology in order to encourage physicians to join their staff. Moreover, some hospitals have provided physicians with low-interest loans for medical offices close to the hospital or have simply built medical offices adjacent to the hospital. The location of these offices tends to encourage admissions by physicians to the nearby hospital.

There are other ways that hospitals convey information besides overt advertising. Names, for instance, can be instructive. The designation "university" in a hospital's name may connote a degree of quality to potential patients. Well-known names like Cleveland Clinic and Mayo Clinic also convey certain quality standards. The reputations associated with these names may be akin to the reputational trademarks of "Coke," "Sanka," or "Kleenex" that one finds in other industries.

The Joint Commission on Accreditation of Healthcare Organizations (JCAHO) (formerly the Joint Commission on Accreditation of Hospitals) has not published any data on how quality of care differs among hospitals. In fact, by extending accreditation to more than 5,000 hospitals, it has helped perpetuate the myth that all hospitals are of equal quality. This is not surprising. The 22-member board of governors of the JCAHO consists of members of the American Medical Association, the American Hospital Association, the American College of Physicians, the American College of Surgeons, and the American Dental Association, along with one public member. The JCAHO's accreditation procedures do not even use outcome measures of hospitals; they rely simply on the inputs and processes of hospital care as measures of performance. Fortunately, the role of the JCAHO appears to be changing. The accrediting body has now pledged to assess hospitals based on outcome measures, at some future date, but whether the JCAHO can be independent from its members is open to question.

It is unclear why third-party insurers have not generally provided information on quality. In addition to the fact that hospital care is complex to measure, the failure may stem from the passive role that insurers previously played in the hospital marketplace—that of paying providers' bills. Further, in its initial years the Blue Cross board of directors was controlled by hospitals, and it was not in the interest of providers to make comparisons among hospitals.

As a more competitive health care system evolves, insurers may assume the responsibility of providing cost and quality information to patients. If an insurer provides incentives for individuals to use the better-quality hospitals, for example, it is possible that some benefits will accrue to the insurer. First, it is possible that quality of care and cost may be inversely related, such that if individuals go to the better-quality hospitals the costs to the insurer can be reduced. Second, it is possible that costs can be reduced if individuals can avoid follow-up care, which may be needed if poor care is initially provided. Third, individuals may be attracted to an insurance firm if they believe that the firm can advise them on the better hospitals. The Prudential Insurance Company's policy of paying for heart, liver, and kidney transplants only at certain quality-approved transplant centers in the United States appears to be a confirmation of these incentives (*Health Care Competition Week* 1990).

It is not clear why federal or state governments or consumer organizations rarely rate hospitals, especially in view of the reluctance of hospitals to advertise directly to patients or to third-party payers. Perhaps the failure of government, private-sector third parties, and consumer organizations to provide information on quality may provide a clue as to why providers did not disseminate such information. Prior to the deregulatory movement in the early 1980s and the era of consumer choice of health plans, consumers did not demand the dissemination of information. That fact, and the complex nature of the information itself, may well account for how little effort and how few resources were expended to measure quality of care.

Differences in Quality among Hospitals

Quality of care seems to differ among hospitals. In cardiac surgery, for example, there appear to be differences based on the number of procedures performed. Luft, Bunker, and Enthoven (1979) found that hospitals doing higher volumes of cardiac surgery had lower in-hospital mortality rates (adjusted for case mix). Moreover, it has been found that 55 percent of the U.S. hospitals that perform cardiac surgery do fewer than 200 cardiac surgeries a year—the minimum number recommended by the Department of Health and Human Services (Kennedy et al. 1982). For cholecystectomies and some types of orthopedic surgery, the number of surgeries performed appears to be inversely related to mortality rates (Luft, Bunker, and Enthoven 1979). Kelly and Hellinger (1986) have suggested that the volume–mortality rate relationship is not physician specific but a function of hospital volume. The December 1987 release of unadjusted mortality rates by the Health Care Financing Administration showed wide differences in mortality rates among hospitals in general as well as for 16 categories of diseases, although these data were not adjusted by case mix (Pear 1987).

The Effect of an Absence of Information on Quality

A reimbursement mechanism based on price or costs alone may result in a reduction in quality of hospital care since hospitals may have incentives to compete by reducing quality. Citing the used-automobile market as an example, Akerlof (1970) illustrates why quality might decline. Akerlof notes that the quality of used automobiles is difficult for the consumer to ascertain. Sellers of used automobiles, therefore, will not spend funds to improve the quality of their automobiles since consumers have a hard time recognizing the better quality automobiles. Indeed, there may be incentives to allow quality to deteriorate. Sellers of used cars will have incentives to compete on a price basis only. A decline in the overall quality of used automobiles may take place.

Given a lack of information on the quality of hospitals, one would expect the quality of hospitals to be less relative to what quality would be with more information. If there were more information on quality, there would be increased incentives for hospitals to compete on a quality basis. Hospitals would be motivated not only by professional standards but by the prospect of achieving an increased market share.

Quality may be a difficult attribute to measure. But perhaps those hospitals on the tail end of the distribution of all hospitals might be good candidates. For example, in California in 1980, 18 hospitals of the 82 that performed adult open-heart surgery did fewer than 100 such surgeries a year (American Hospital Association 1981). In view of the Department of Health and Human Services standards of at least 200 cardiac surgeries a year, the 18 hospitals might be deemed suboptimal unless there were additional medical evidence to the contrary.

One would also expect an absence of information on quality to affect patient selection of hospitals. Individuals go to particular hospitals for a number of reasons. There may be a religious attachment such that an individual feels more at ease in a hospital sponsored by his or her religion. Convenience may be a factor; the costs of transportation and lodging for a patient and patient's family may be substantial for individuals hospitalized far from home. An individual may go to a hospital because of a particular physician or surgeon who has been recommended by other patients or physicians. Successful prior hospitalization may prompt another visit to the original hospital when the need arises. An individual may also belong to a health maintenance organization or preferred provider organization that only fully reimburses affiliated hospitals. In emergency cases patients may go to the most convenient hospital notwithstanding its quality. Finally, a patient may enter a hospital on the advice of his or her physician.

Effective Dissemination of Information on Quality

Information dissemination by hospitals

Antitrust laws should be enforced by the Justice Department and the Federal Trade Commission at the national level and by the antitrust authorities at the state level to ensure that there are no barriers, implicit or explicit, to providing information on the quality of hospital care by hospitals. Hospitals spend more than $1 billion a year on advertising (Steiber 1986). It is possible that the costs of increased advertising may be reflected in higher prices of health care. It is also possible, however, that like many industries, the hospital industry will find the costs of increased advertising counterbalanced by the economies of scale made possible by increased market share.

Information dissemination by government

One example of information dissemination by government is the release in December 1987 of mortality rates for 5,971 short-term, acute care hospitals that treated Medicare beneficiaries in 1986. Comments from hospitals on the accuracy and meaningfulness of the data were released in the same report. Mortality rates for each hospital as a whole were published as well as mortality rates for 16 high- and low-risk medical conditions. Among these conditions were severe acute heart disease, pulmonary disease, renal disease, low-risk heart disease, and ophthalmic diseases. Although the data for each hospital's mortality rate did not take into consideration patients' severity of illness, race, and family income, the data were adjusted for patients' age, sex, secondary ailments, and previous hospital admissions.

Three important benefits accrued to potential patients with the release of these mortality data. First, the report allowed potential patients to understand that there may be differences in quality of care among hospitals as there are differences in the quality of goods and services among firms in any industry. Second, hospitals could use these data in their advertising, which would further spark individuals' awareness of differences among hospitals. Finally, third-party payers could use these data to help their enrollees choose the hospital with the most appropriate mix of quality and cost.

It would be difficult, however, for patients to base their selection of a hospital solely on the government data. These mortality data are not adjusted for severity of illness; thus, a hospital may have a high mortality rate simply because it has attracted individuals who are much sicker relative to those admitted to other hospitals. Further, the data are broken out into only 16 broad categories. It is possible, for example, for someone with pulmonary disease to have one of hundreds of different types of pulmonary conditions. A hospital may excel in treating a particular type of pulmonary disease yet perform poorly in treating another type. These treatment differences would not be detected in the current data. In addition, since patients may have illnesses that require hospitalization only from time to time, they would have to rely on data that might be obsolete at the time they are ready to enter the hospital.

Information dissemination by physicians

Individuals must be admitted to hospitals by physicians. Although a patient's preference for a familiar or conveniently located hospital may influence a physician's decision, a physician's referral is necessary.

Suppose, however, that physicians could be held liable for the hospital to which they referred patients. Suppose that, if an unsatisfactory outcome occurred, the referring physician would bear legal responsibility in the same way that under the malpractice laws physicians may bear legal responsibility for providing diagnoses outside the bounds of generally accepted medical practice. Physicians would then have incentives to send individuals to quality hospitals consistent with the priorities of convenience and other attributes desired by the patient.

Physicians should know which are the better hospitals in the same way that any member of any profession or organization knows who are the superior members. Indeed, a major reason why patients go to physicians is to seek information and advice from an informed professional. It is, of course, possible that physicians may be unaware of the precise mortality rate of particular hospitals. It is also possible that there may be disagreements among physicians on the rankings of quality of various hospitals. Yet, most professors can identify Harvard, Yale, and Princeton as among the superior universities although there may be disagreement about their relative rankings.

Physicians' behavior might change if they were liable for hospital referrals. To avoid potential litigation, perhaps the physician might offer the patient a choice of a few hospitals, along with an explanation of the relative merits of each. A physician might also explain that he or she has staff privileges at one or more of the hospitals and the nature of any potential financial conflicts associated with the referral. For example, physicians with such privileges at a particular hospital would be able to attend the patients they referred there and thus gain additional income. On the other hand, continuity of care may be strengthened by an individual's physician attending him or her at the hospital.

If physicians were liable for hospital referrals, hospitals of suboptimal quality would lose patients and might have to eliminate or close their poorer departments. Hospitals of superior quality would attract a greater number of patients. Moreover, health care costs might be reduced since the fixed costs of surgery or other procedures at the better hospitals could be spread over a greater number of patients and economies of scale would be realized. In addition, the current problem of surplus hospital beds and excess capacity could be solved not by certificate-of-need regulations, by which government agencies decide which hospitals can compete or expand in the marketplace, but by allowing the physician to be the patient's advocate.

In certain rural areas where there may be only a few hospitals, the closure of one or more hospitals might present a problem of reduced access to care. It is not clear that each area needs a sophisticated hospital unit, but the costs of reduced access such as increased transportation costs must be balanced against the potential for reducing the costs of all hospital care that increased specialization may provide (Schwartz and Joskow 1980).

There might be some governmental actions that would complement a physician-liability rule. For example, physicians might be required to reveal any financial conflicts of interest associated with a hospital referral. This would not be unlike the current promulgations of the Council on Ethical and Judicial Affairs of the American Medical Association, which maintain that a physician "should not be influenced in the prescribing of drugs, devices or appliances by a direct or indirect financial interest in a pharmaceutical firm or other supplier" (American Medical Association 1986, 30–31)

Information dissemination by third-party insurers

Third parties could offer new insurance plans to complement a physician-liability rule. Such plans might require, for example, a fully reimbursed second or third opinion for choice of hospital for serious surgery. In this way, like second-opinion programs for elective surgery, a patient would receive the opinion of an additional physician who might not have any financial conflict with the recommended hospital. Further, one would expect that third parties would begin to compile and distribute to their enrollees data on the quality of care. Third parties would act as brokers between hospitals and patients by interpreting the quality of care of hospitals for prospective patients. Third-party insurers have the advantage of a data base of a large number of insured who go to area hospitals for a number of different conditions.

The Long-Run Effect of Improved Information Dissemination

I have suggested that, in the short run, the effect of increased information might be to close the poorer departments in hospitals and to increase admissions to hospitals with superior departments. It is also possible that better quality of care—received because of better information on where to find it—would reduce the necessity for subsequent admissions and thus help lower costs. Economies of scale could be achieved, which would reduce costs as well. These reductions in costs, however, would have to be balanced against possible reductions in access.

If more individuals were well informed about the superior hospitals, a difficult policy dilemma would arise. Increased information in most markets assures that individuals will be able to purchase goods or services based on one's relative preference of price and quality. Some individuals may choose a good of the highest price and quality, for example, while others may choose a good of somewhat lower price and quality. In the hospital marketplace, however, quality is usually given a greater emphasis than price, since third parties pay nearly all of the hospital bill. If, therefore, individuals had increased information on the quality of hospitals, and price was relatively unimportant, how would the superior hospitals—at which demand would be the greatest—allocate beds to patients?

The rationing of care in superior hospitals might be based, in part, on whether patients could afford the price of hospital services and the travel costs, such as transportation and lodging for out-of-town patients. Hospitals could raise the price of some services not fully covered by insurance. Patients unable to afford the services might be denied hospitalization at superior hospitals.

Rationing could also take the form of greater copayments for hospitalization at the superior hospitals. Government or private insurers could also refuse to pay for hospitalizations for individuals over the age of, say, 85 at superior hospitals. Superior hospitals might also elect to accept only the most difficult and interesting cases.

It should be understood, of course, that superior hospital care is currently rationed. Individuals at lower socioeconomic levels may be less educated and more intimidated by physicians and consider fewer alternative hospitals than individuals at higher socioeconomic levels. Thus it is possible that lower-income individuals already receive a greater proportion of their care at the poorer hospitals (Inguanzo and Harju 1985). Anyone concerned about achieving equity in health care would be remiss not to consider the relative quality of hospital care that individuals receive.

There are two additional implications of increased information on the quality of care of hospitals. First, because increased information would drive some hospitals out of business, the remaining hospitals could have greater monopoly power because of higher market share. Often, firms use monopoly power to raise their prices. Therefore, an increase in price must be balanced against a potential increase in quality of care as well as increased economies of scale.

Second, if hospitals begin to advertise their quality-of-care attributes, there is always the possibility of deceptive advertising, despite the Federal Trade Commission Act sanction against unfair or deceptive acts or practices. Deceptive advertising is conceivable in this industry because hospital services are complex. In the health care sector, there have already been Federal Trade Commission actions against firms that made unsubstantiated claims about the efficacy of diet products and hair implants as well as against chiropractors who advertised the effectiveness of "laser facelifts" (*Dardus* 1984). The Federal Trade Commission will need to examine carefully the costs and benefits of bringing consumer protection complaints against potential deceptive advertising in the hospital industry.

References

Akerlof, G. A. (1970). "The Market for 'Lemons': Quality, Uncertainty and the Market Mechanism," *Quarterly Journal of Economics* 84: 488–500.

American Hospital Association (1977). *Guidelines—Advertising by Hospitals.* Chicago: The Association.

American Hospital Association (1987). *Hospital Statistics.* Chicago: The Association.

American Hospital Association (1981). *Hospitals with Open-Heart or Cardiac Catherization Facilities.* Chicago: The Association.

American Medical Association, Council on Ethical and Judicial Affairs (1986). *Current Opinions of the Council on Ethical and Judicial Affairs of the American Medical Association—1986.* Chicago: The Association.

Bazzolli, G. (1986). "Health Care for the Indigent: Overview of Critical Issues," *Health Services Research* 21 (no. 3): 353-93.

Thomas A. Dardus, 3 Trade Reg. Rep. (CCH) 22172 (FTC C-3144 1984) (Consent Order); *Hair Extension of Beverly Hills, Inc.*, 95 FTC 361 (1980) (Consent Order) and *Terrance D. Lesko, M.D.*, 96 FTC 73 (1980) (Consent Order); *Adria Laboratories, Inc.*, 103 FTC 512 (1984) (Consent Order); *Spinal Health Services, Inc.*, 102 FTC 1319 (1983) (Consent Order).

Ermann, D., and Gabel, J. (1984). "Multihospital Systems: Issues and Empirical Findings," *Health Affairs* 3: 51–64.

Fanara, P., Jr., and Greenberg, W. (1985). "Factors Affecting the Adoption of Prospective Reimbursement Programs by State Governments." In *Incentives Vs. Controls in Health Policy,* ed. J.Meyer, 144–56. Washington, DC: American Enterprise Institute.

Gaul, G. M. (1986). "Pennsylvania Consumers Soon to Get Detailed Health Data," *The Philadelphia Inquirer* (July 3): B-1, B-7.

Gaumer, G. (1986). "Medicare Patient Outcomes and Hospital Organizational Mission." In *For-Profit Enterprise in Health Care,* ed. B. Gray, 354–74. Washington, DC: National Academy Press.

Greenberg, W. (1986). "The Evolution of Blue Cross in a Competitive Marketplace," *Business and Health* 4 (no. 1): 44–47.

Health Care Competition Week (1990). "State and Private Initiatives are Pushing Ahead in the Quest for Quality," 7: 5–8.

Health Care Financing Administration. "National Health Expenditures, 1988." *Health Care Financing Review* 11 (no. 4): 1–41.

Inguanzo, J. M., and Harju, M. (1985). "Affluent Consumers Most Discriminating: Survey," *Hospitals* 59: 84, 86.

Institute of Medicine (1986a). "Changes in Ownership, Control, and Configuration of Health Care Services." In *For-Profit Enterprise in Health Care,* ed. B. Gray, 26–46. Washington, DC: National Academy Press.

———. (1986b). "Implications for Education and Research." In *For-Profit Enterprise in Health Care,* ed. B. Gray, 142–50. Washington, DC: National Academy Press.

Johns, L. (1987). "Selective Contracting for Health Services in California." In *Charting the Future of Health Care,* eds. J. Meyer and M. E. Lewin, 51–73. Washington, DC: American Enterprise Institute.

Johns, L., Anderson, M., and Derzon, R. (1985). "Selective Contracting in California: Experience in the Second Year," *Inquiry* 22: 335–47.

Kelly, J. V., and Hellinger, F. J. (1986). "Physician and Hospital Factors Associated with Mortality of Surgical Patients," *Medical Care* 24: 785–800.

Kennedy, R. H. et al. (1982). "Cardiac-Catheterization and Cardiac-Surgical Facilities," *The New England Journal of Medicine* 307 (no. 16): 986–92.

Luft, H. S., Bunker, J. P., and Enthoven, A. C. (1979). "Should Operations be Regionalized? The Empirical Relation Between Surgical Volume and Mortality," *New England Journal of Medicine* 301: 1364–69.

McCombs, J. S., and Christianson, J. B. (1987). "Applying Competitive Bidding to Health Care," *Journal of Health Politics, Policy and Law* 12 (no. 4): 707–09.

Morrisey, M. A., Sloan, F. A., and Valvona, J. (1988). "Defining Geographic Markets for Hospital Care," *Law and Contemporary Problems* 51 (no. 2): 165–94.

Pattison, R., and Katz, H. (1983). "Investor-Owned and Not-For-Profit Hospitals: A Comparison Based on California Data," *New England Journal of Medicine* 309 (no. 6): 347–53.

Pear, R. (1987). "Mortality Data Released for 6,000 U.S. Hospitals," *The New York Times* (December 18): B-5.

Prospective Payment Assessment Commission (1985). *Technical Appendixes to the Report and Recommendations to the Secretary, U.S. Department of Health and Human Services,* April 1, 1985, p. 9.

Relman, A. (1980). "The New Medical-Industrial Complex," *The New England Journal of Medicine* 303 (no. 17): 963–70.

Salkever, David S. (1978). "Competition Among Hospitals." In *Competition in the Health Care Sector: Past Present and Future,* ed. W. Greenberg, 149–61. Rockville, MD: Aspen System Corporation.

Salkever, D. S., and Bice, T. (1976). "The Impact of Certificate-of-Need Controls on Hospital Investment," *Milbank Memorial Fund Quarterly/Health and Society* 54 (no. 2): 185–214.

Schwartz, W., and Joskow, P. (1980). "Duplicated Hospital Facilities: How Much Can We Save by Consolidating Them?" *New England Journal of Medicine* 303 (no. 25): 1449–57.

Shortell, S. M. (1986). "Implication of Hospital Ownership on Access to Care." In *The For-Profit Hospital,* eds. R. F. Southby and W. Greenberg, 128–41. Columbus, OH: Battelle Press.

Sloan, F., and Vraciu, R. (1983). "Invester-Owned and Not-for-Profit Hospitals: Addressing Some Issues," *Health Affairs* 2 (no. 1): 25–37.

Steiber, S. R. (1986). "$1.1 Billion Spent on Hospital Marketing in 1986," *Hospitals* 60 (no. 22): 64.

Stigler, G. J. (1971). "The Theory of Economic Regulation," *Bell Journal of Economics* 2: 3–21.

Townsend, J. (1986). "Hospitals and Their Communities: A Report on Three Case Studies." In *For-Profit Enterprise in Health Care,* ed. B. Gray, 458–73. Washington, DC: Institute of Medicine, National Academy Press.

U.S. Bureau of the Census (1968). *Statistical Abstract of the United States,* 1968, 89th Edition. Table 82, p. 64. Washington, DC: U.S. Government Printing Office.

U.S. Bureau of the Census (1990). *Statistical Abstract of the United States,* 1990, 110th Edition. Table 163, p. 105. Washington, DC: U.S. Government Printing Office.

Washington Post (1984). "I Never Thought Twice about Which Hospital Has the Best Heart Program," (December 17): B-6.

4

Health Insurance and the Uninsured

During the last decade, insuring organizations such as Blue Cross and Blue Shield, the commercial carriers, third-party administrators, health maintenance organizations, and preferred provider organizations—in short, the private insurance industry—have paid approximately 70 percent of U.S. health care expenses. This chapter will review the incentives, structure, and behavior of Blue Cross and Blue Shield, the commercial insurers, and third-party administrators in the private sector, as well as discuss that portion of the population that is uninsured. Chapter 5 will discuss health maintenance organizations and preferred provider organizations. Chapter 6 will review the Medicare and Medicaid health insurance programs in the public sector.

Insurance in non-health care sectors of the economy may be a significant factor in the payment of losses. There is one important difference, however, between insurance in the health care sector and insurance in other sectors: in health care, insurance involves the potential problem of moral hazard. Moral hazard is the increased use of services by the insured party due to the fact that the insurance services are covered by insurance. In contrast, moral hazard is rarely present with other types of insurance (Pauly 1968). Individuals by and large do not increase their consumption of non–health care services when the services are insured.

The purchase of insurance appears to be rational for protection against uncertain, large expenditures (or losses). In health care, however, many individuals have traditionally had insurance that would cover even modest expenses.

Most economists believe that the nation's tax laws have contributed to this demand for first-dollar coverage in health care (Feldstein

1973). Health insurance premiums paid by employers are not subject to federal, state, local, or social security taxes. Employer-paid health insurance is especially significant since approximately 80 percent of individuals in the private sector receive insurance coverage from their employers (Health Insurance Association of America 1990). The resistance of governments to imposing taxes on any insurance premiums paid by the employer creates incentives for individuals to demand more untaxed health insurance (including insurance for minor, inexpensive services such as teeth cleaning) relative to taxable wages or salaries. Employers have catered to this demand in the competition to hire employees.

With the large reduction in federal tax rates in the 1980s, insurance coverage for inexpensive health services became less attractive to employees. It is not surprising, then, that there was a movement away from complete coverage—although undoubtedly other factors, such as rising health care expenses, also made employers less likely to pay for full coverage. Further, rising health care expenses created incentives for employers to demand that insurers take a more active role in cost containment. Employers must balance their interest in reducing health care costs with their interest in attracting employees through a health care benefit package competitive with benefit packages offered by other employers.

Insurance and Rising Prices

The presence of insurance in health care makes the patient less sensitive to the prices charged by the providers of services. The demand for health care services thus becomes less elastic or less responsive to price in the presence of insurance. Insurance also shifts the demand curve to the right, increasing the demand for health care services. This phenomenon puts upward pressure on the prices of health care services at the same time it increases the amount of health care services used. Moreover, because of insurance, patients have less incentive to search for the lowest price for any given service, which lessens any tendency for providers to reduce prices. In addition, it is possible that with patients who are insensitive to price, providers may adopt new, more expensive technology, which will put continual upward pressure on prices and utilization (Newhouse 1988).

Types of Insuring Organizations

A number of organizations provide health insurance in the United States. They vary in their historical background, organizational form, size, ability to accept risks, and potential ability to contain costs.

Blue Cross and Blue Shield

Before the Great Depression, individuals would receive hospital care but be unable to pay for it. Consequently, in 1929 hospitals formed the Blue Cross organization so that individuals could pay a set monthly premium, in advance of any hospitalization, which would cover all hospital costs (Eilers 1963). The existence of Blue Cross reduced the amount of bad debt that hospitals had to incur.

Blue Shield was begun in the early 1920s. Before its formation, there were a number of industrywide health insurance plans in railroading, logging, and mining, and the plans were aggressive in containing costs, including the costs of physician services (Goldberg and Greenberg 1977). Physicians, concerned about such cost containment, formed their own health insurance firms. By promoting their own insurance firms and refusing to accept payment from the more cost-conscious insurers, the physicians soon put an end to the more aggressive tactics of the health insurance plans that were not dominated by physicians. The American Medical Association endorsed the physician-sponsored plans and helped integrate some of the plans into Blue Shield plans in the middle 1940s (U.S. Federal Trade Commission 1979). With the formation of Blue Shield, physicians controlled their own insurance plans—plans that paid for physician services yet paid little attention to cost containment.

By 1980 there were 69 active Blue Shield plans in the United States. At least one physician sat on the board of directors of each plan, and in many plans physicians constituted board majorities (Greenberg 1981, 364). Due to cost-containment pressures and Federal Trade Commission enforcement activities, physicians began to relinquish control of Blue Shield boards during the 1980s. By the late 1980s, Blue Shield was more concerned with surviving in the marketplace than with pleasing physicians.

Both Blue Cross and Blue Shield were organized as nonprofit entities. As such, the plans have generally been exempt from federal and state income taxes as well as from property taxes. In nearly all areas of the United States, the Blue Cross and Blue Shield plans are merged. In some states there is more than one Blue Cross plan. In addition, in California, there is a single Blue Cross plan, which sells hospitalization and physician coverage throughout the state, as well as a single Blue Shield plan, which also sells hospitalization and physician coverage throughout the state.

Blue Cross and Blue Shield have had about 50 percent of the traditional indemnity health insurance market (that is, insurance for health care rendered on a fee-for-service basis) since the early 1950s. In 1987 there were 77 Blue Cross and Blue Shield plans, with each plan retaining autonomy in claims-processing and cost-containment procedures.

Commercial insurers

There are approximately 350 commercial firms that sell health insurance in the United States. Commercial health insurers sell insurance in each of the 50 states, although not every firm sells insurance in every state. Nearly all of the large firms also sell insurance in non–health care areas. For example, firms like Travelers, Prudential, and Metropolitan Life have a substantial business in property, automobile, and life insurance. The commercial insurers have typically reimbursed providers on a fee-for-service basis, although many have begun health maintenance organizations and preferred provider organizations.

Why, in comparison with commercial insurers, have Blue Cross and Blue Shield had such a significant share of the health insurance market both across the United States and within many states? For example, their market share in New York State has traditionally been about 75 percent of private-sector insureds and in Rhode Island about 90 percent of private-sector insureds (Goldberg and Greenberg 1985, 720).

The Blues' dominant position may be due to several factors. First, Blue Cross and Blue Shield are nonprofit firms while commercial carriers are for-profit firms. The nonprofit Blue Cross and Blue Shield firms need not pay property tax or federal or state income taxes. The Blues are also exempt from the premium taxes that many states levy and that commercial insurers must pay. As the oldest and best-known health insurers, the Blues may also have name-recognition advantages that individual commercial insurers do not share. On the other hand, the Blues are regulated in nearly every state and may have to offer an open-enrollment period each year, during which anyone may enroll without a medical examination. Some states also require the Blues to cover preexisting conditions after a specified time period. These regulations may subject the Blues to enrollment by individuals who are more seriously ill than those who enroll with commercial carriers.

Blue Cross and Blue Shield, perhaps by virtue of its size and bargaining power with hospitals, has also secured a discount on charges from hospitals in nearly every state. In some states the discount is as high as 25 percent. The individual commercial insurer has a market share too small to secure such a discount, thus yielding a cost advantage to Blue Cross and Blue Shield (Goldberg and Greenberg 1985, 720).

Blue Cross and Blue Shield plans do not usually compete against one another in a particular geographic area. The effect of these market divisions might be to make prices higher than would be the case if there were no segmentation. The arrangement is analogous to an agreement among automobile dealers representing the same manufacturer that each dealership will serve only customers from its own area, eliminating geographic competition among dealers.

Insurers' Incentives to Contain Costs

Blue Cross and Blue Shield and commercial insurers have incentives to contain health care costs just as a manufacturing firm has incentives to minimize its costs. If one insuring organization has greater expenditures for hospital and physician care than its competitors, it will lose market share. Before the 1980s, however, the Blues made little or no effort to contain costs. They paid hospitals their costs (less any discount on charges) without regard to utilization of services. Physicians were reimbursed on a usual, customary, and reasonable basis; that is, physicians received payment for procedures based on the lower of their usual charge or the customary charge of all physicians with a similar professional and geographic profile. Under the usual, customary, and reasonable scheme, however, physicians had little to lose by submitting a higher fee to Blue Shield since they could always collect the customary fee. Indeed, the customary fee schedule increased each time a physician submitted a higher fee. Furthermore, there was rarely a check on the number of procedures performed by physicians or the amount of hospitalization that may actually have been necessary.

Blue Shield often used a participation program such that if physicians participated directly with Blue Shield, Blue Shield reimbursed them directly. If physicians elected not to participate, Blue Shield would reimburse the patient who in turn would pay the physician. A copayment was usually instituted to help curtail utilization.

Commercial carriers generally reimburse the patient directly and have larger deductibles and higher copayments than do Blue Cross and Blue Shield plans (Frech and Ginsburg 1978). Like the Blues, commercial carriers have rarely attempted to contain excessive utilization or provider fees.

One should be aware of the incentives of insuring organizations to understand why they have not been more aggressive in containing cost. An insuring organization must operate within the conflicting incentives of the employer, the patient, and the physician. The employer has incentives to contain costs, since health care costs reduce the profitability of the firm. The employer also has incentives to attract the most productive employees; one way to attract employees is to offer an attractive health benefit package with few out-of-pocket expenses that the employee believes will not compromise quality of care. If a benefit package has cost-containment provisions that are too restrictive, physicians may complain to patients that quality of care has been reduced. Patient dissatisfaction with the benefit package would impinge on employer-employee relations.

The benefit package that would be least problematic in terms of relationships with employees and physicians is a comprehensive benefit package that does not curtail a physician's utilization decisions; this package would also engender the highest health care costs. At some point, however, the increased costs of health care may outweigh the complaints of employees and physicians. In addition, health care costs remain an opportunity cost to the payment of increased wages or benefits that might otherwise be paid to employees.

Self-Insured Health Plans

The health insurance industry also includes firms that do not perform the traditional insurance function but, instead, only administer health plans for employer groups. In this case, the employers elect to self-insure for health care expenditures in the belief that they are large enough to anticipate and to pay out-of-pocket the yearly health care costs their employees incur. More than 175,000 employers chose to self-insure in 1986, and more than half of the country's employees participated in such plans (McDonnell, Gutenberg, Greenberg, and Arnott 1986). Blue Cross and Blue Shield and the commercial carriers administered 26 percent of these plans, third-party administrators (small-sized claims administrators who are not identified with Blue Cross and Blue Shield or the commercial carriers) managed

51 percent, and 23 percent administered their own plans (McDonnell, Gutenberg, Greenberg, and Arnott 1986). This suggests that third-party administrators have a significant presence in the marketplace and compete with Blue Cross and Blue Shield, the commercial carriers, and alternative delivery systems. Moreover, the employer's option to self-insure can exert competitive pressure on insuring organizations to reduce their premiums.

There are a number of reasons why employers elect to self-insure. First, firms may save the administrative costs of retaining a large insurance firm when they are reasonably able to anticipate potential losses among their own employees. This is especially true among the larger employers, which are much less affected by unusually high expenses incurred by only a few employees. The percentage of employers who self-insure increases with firm size (McDonnell, Gutenberg, Greenberg, and Arnott 1986). Second, the Employee Retirement and Income Security Act of 1974 (PL 93–406) exempts self-insured health plans from many state laws that mandate particular benefits. States may, for example, mandate coverage of psychiatric or home care, a requirement that may increase insurers' premiums, and hence the non-self-insuring employer's costs, by a considerable amount. Third, employers pay no state premium taxes if they self-insure; these taxes run as high as 2 percent of premiums. Fourth, self-insured health plans are exempt from the requirement that they maintain certain reserves for claims that are unpaid or unreported (McDonnell, Gutenberg, Greenberg, and Arnott 1986, 2).

The Changing Nature of Insurance and the Uninsured

One of the most dramatic changes in the health care sector in the 1980s was that insuring organizations no longer simply paid the bills of providers but became more aggressive in cost containment. Although this chapter will concentrate only on the activities of the private-sector insurers, Medicare and Medicaid in the public sector also became much more aggressive in cost containment. (Insurers have not always been passive in their cost-containment efforts. Dental insurers have attempted to contain costs, for example, by requesting x-rays from dentists before authorizing treatment. Less costly forms of treatment may be suggested from these x-rays. It may be easier, however, for dental insurers to monitor costs than health insurers since there may be less uncertainty in dentistry than in medicine about the most appropriate procedures to be used (Greenberg 1981).)

Insurers, unlike most individual purchasers of health care services, may have substantial information about the fees and utilization patterns of an entire array of providers for a given procedure. Insurers, therefore, should be able to ascertain if the fees charged by particular providers are excessive. In addition, from their knowledge of treatment patterns for individuals with similar diagnoses, insurers should be able to ascertain if the tests given to patients are appropriate and whether patients' hospital admissions and lengths of stay are warranted.

No insurer will be able to make these calculations with absolute precision (patients' health status and physicians' practice patterns may vary considerably), but an insurer with a large number of enrollees may be able to calculate the expected costs of an illness within specific, reasonable ranges. In contrast, an individual patient may have a particular illness only once in a lifetime and thus may have very little idea of physician fees or the total cost of the illness. The DRG system is an example of an insuring organization using its information on a large number of diagnoses in order to contain costs—in this case by setting maximum expenditure limits. In this way, health care insurers can lessen the asymmetry of information about fees and procedures that has long existed between the patient and the provider.

Insuring organizations may also have bargaining power with providers that individuals do not have. One reason that Medicare can implement the DRG system is that Medicare accounts for such a large share of the income of the providers. If Medicare payment were refused, providers would find it difficult to recoup the loss of market share. Blue Cross and Blue Shield is able to secure large discounts on charges from hospitals for the same reason (Frech and Ginsburg 1988). A single individual does not have such bargaining power.

Cost containment by third-party insurers

Cost containment by third-party insurers may be broken into three different components. First, insurers may structure benefit packages in such a way as to put some of the cost containment burden on the patient. This may be accomplished through copayments or deductibles, in which case the patient is responsible for some or all of the bill. The benefit package may also emphasize the provision of care in settings that tend to be less costly, such as outpatient surgery, or require second opinions for elective surgery. The benefit package may create incentives to use low-cost providers, incentives that are usually a hallmark of the preferred provider organization. Finally, the benefit package may not include payment for particular procedures such as heart transplants or experimental surgeries.

Insurers' second cost-containment strategy may take the form of monitoring the fees and utilization patterns of individual physicians. Utilization review is one of the most common means insuring organizations use to control the costs of individual physicians. It may consist of preadmission certification, which requires permission from the insurer before a patient can be admitted to the hospital; concurrent review, whereby the insurer monitors length of stay while a patient is in the hospital; or retrospective review, which takes place after the patient has been discharged.

As costs have steadily grown in recent years, both Blue Cross and Blue Shield and the commercial carriers have intensified their cost-containment efforts. Nearly all Blue Cross and Blue Shield plans and commercial carriers offer a managed care option to potential enrollees. Under the managed care option, health insurance plans may require second opinions for elective surgery, as well as utilization reviews. In this way, the attending physician is circumscribed in his or her decision-making capability by the financial and quality concerns of the health insurers. The ultimate forms of managed care are the preferred provider organizations and health maintenance organizations which are described in the following chapter.

Although utilization review may have a deterrent effect on physicians, it may be ineffective in controlling procedures or tests that yield some marginal benefits to the patient, yet whose costs exceed the benefits. The third-party payer will have to accept these costs if it wants to avoid responsibility for any adverse outcomes (Goldberg and Greenberg 1988). Feldstein, Wickizer, and Wheeler (1988), however, have suggested that utilization review may have a significant effect on hospital utilization and total medical expenditures

The third means by which insuring organizations attempt to contain costs is the selection of only the lowest cost providers from among those submitting competitive bids. For example, only hospitals with the lowest cost per case, adjusted for differences in types of cases treated, would be acceptable to the insuring organization. Adequate access to the hospitals chosen would also have been taken into consideration (Johns, Anderson, and Derzon 1985).

Avoiding high-risk individuals

In addition to engaging in cost-containment strategies, insuring organizations may try to identify and avoid the enrollment of individuals who are especially likely to incur large medical bills in the foreseeable future. An insurer that does not enroll individuals with large medical bills may have distinct cost advantages over its competitors. Generally, however, individuals are very knowledgeable about their health status, whereas the insuring organization is not.

Insurers have attempted to reduce this asymmetry of information in a number of ways. One way is to exclude preexisting conditions from health care coverage. For example, many insuring organizations have declined to cover individual applicants (applicants who are not members of, for example, employee groups) who have acquired immune deficiency syndrome (AIDS) or who test positive for the human immunodeficiency virus (HIV) infection (Greenberg 1989). Another way to avoid the enrollment of high-risk individuals is for insuring organizations to design their benefit packages to attract the most favorable risks. For example, well-baby and dental care provisions in a benefit package might attract younger families. High deductibles and high copayments (and the resultant lower premiums) might attract persons who expect their out-of-pocket expenses to be low because they rarely use services. Insuring organizations may also advertise in media that may be seen by young, single individuals.

Insuring organizations may not sell coverage in certain geographic areas or to employer groups in which individuals with diseases such as AIDS are common. Individuals who are not members of an employer group might also be deemed to be undesirable risks since they might be too ill to hold a job. In addition, the administrative costs of enrolling individuals without a group connection may increase health care premiums, reducing the demand for such insurance.

As an alternative to not enrolling high-risk individuals, it is possible that insuring organizations could increase their premiums to take into account the expected future health care costs of high-risk enrollees. In many states, however, insurance commissions regulate Blue Cross and Blue Shield premiums for nongroup individuals. Since an increase in premiums is ruled out in these states, the Blues plans there may ignore the enrollment of nongroup individuals to a greater extent than if premiums were allowed to increase (Fanara and Greenberg 1985). Moreover, it may be difficult for non-Blues plans to achieve an equilibrium price (at which supply equals demand) when they must charge higher premiums to cover expected losses. A full benefit package at a higher price will attract only the sickest individuals. This will drive the price of the benefit package still higher. Economists have shown that a stable equilibrium price cannot even exist under these circumstances (Rothschild and Stiglitz 1976). Eventually, firms will remove themselves from this segment of the insurance marketplace as many firms already have in nongroup markets (Office of Technology Assessment 1988).

The Uninsured

Those who cannot obtain health insurance coverage because they are at high risk are among approximately 37 million individuals in this country who have no health insurance. The others in this group lack insurance because they cannot afford it or because their employers do not offer it.

There are four main reasons why employers do not offer health insurance to their employees. First, health insurance premiums are costs that employers must pay, in the same way that employers pay wages. Health insurance premiums represent opportunity costs, and a firm may believe it can spend its money more productively on increased wages or increased capital investment for the firm than on health insurance. Second, firms may believe their employees can always get medical attention at public hospitals, which must accept all patients regardless of ability to pay. Firms not financing health insurance in any form have a competitive advantage over firms incurring the expense of health care coverage. Third, firms may employ individuals who value increased wages more highly than increased health care benefits. Finally, health-insuring organizations may not want to sell insurance to what they consider to be high-risk employer groups.

In addition to those who do not have health insurance, there are a large number of individuals who are underinsured. Underinsurance is a term that is difficult to define precisely, but some economists suggest that it may be defined as a function of the probability (for example, 1 percent to 5 percent) that out-of-pocket medical expenses will be greater than, say, 10 percent of family income. Current estimates indicate that approximately 13 percent of the privately insured population under age 65 is underinsured (Farley 1985).

Who are the uninsured?

In 1985, more than one-eighth of the U.S. population had no health insurance. Moreover, the number of uninsured in absolute terms and as a percentage of the U.S. population has increased substantially since 1970 (Wilensky 1988, 137).

Although most of the U.S. population receives its private health insurance coverage from employers, a brief from the Employee Benefit

Research Institute (EBRI) (1987) reports that two-thirds of those without coverage are full-time, full-year workers or reside in families headed by full-time, full-year workers. EBRI reports also that more than half of the working uninsured are employed in retail trade or in service industries and that a large proportion, or 24 percent, of self-employed workers do not have health insurance. Within employer groups, one finds fewer employees covered in the smaller firms, and most workers in employer groups without health insurance are in low-income categories. Approximately three-quarters of the 24 million employed individuals without health insurance have incomes of less than $10,000 a year, although they live in families whose incomes are greater than three times the U.S. poverty level (Swartz 1990). Many of these employed individuals are also young—more than half are between the ages of 18 and 34 (Swartz 1990).

The amount of time that individuals are without health insurance is also of interest. Swartz and McBride (1990) found, for example, that only 50 percent of the uninsured are without insurance for more than four months. Those who are without health insurance for the longest time are individuals who are unemployed or out of the labor force.

Evidence suggests that the uninsured have, as would be predicted, reduced access to the health care system. They see physicians only two-thirds as often as the insured. They also make greater use of emergency rooms and hospital outpatient departments and average only three-quarters as many days in the hospital (Brown 1990).

In a large nationwide study that attempted to control for clinical status, Hadley, Steinberg, and Feder (1991) found that uninsured individuals compared to privately insured patients had conditions of higher risk when admitted to hospitals and had shorter lengths of stay. In addition, while in the hospital, uninsured individuals had fewer high-cost or high-discretion procedures, such as coronary artery bypass surgery. The uninsured, adjusted for case mix, also had a higher mortality rate than privately insured patient.

In summary, access appears to be reduced for the uninsured relative to the insured population. And, while the uninsured are in the hospital, it appears that providers may render them a lower level of care.

Health care as a merit good

Many people would term health care a merit good, like adequate housing and an adequate diet. Merit goods are goods and services that society generally believes should be provided regardless of one's ability to afford them. To ensure such a good or service is provided, society must make a value judgment on the amount of it that constitutes a merit good and therefore ought to be provided at little or no cost. In the case of housing and food, our society has made judgments such that more than 2 million people receive low-income housing assistance and more than 21 million people receive food stamps (U.S. Bureau of the Census 1988, 444).

In the case of health care, most everyone would agree that all persons should have access to emergency care. Not everyone, however, would agree that an entire population should be entitled to health care assistance for every ailment. Assuming a consensus that at least some health care assistance should be provided for those who cannot afford it or obtain it, what are the policy options for the distribution of such assistance?

Policy Options

Five options to provide health care coverage for uninsured individuals will be discussed in this section. Three of the options—the formation of risk pools, the subsidization of insurers who enroll high-risk individuals, and the expansion of Medicaid—involve increased government financing of health care. The other two options—regulation of Blue Cross and Blue Shield and expansion of employer-offered health insurance—may involve increased government regulation but may not necessitate increased government financing of health care. A sixth option, elimination of employer-based health insurance, will be discussed in Chapter 11.

Formation of risk pools

Many states have risk pools for medically high-risk individuals. These pools are conceptually similar to the risk pools available to drivers who are at a major risk for automobile accidents. People who have been denied health coverage by insuring organizations and who are not eligible for coverage from Medicare or Medicaid are usually eligible for enrollment in risk pools. Generally, a state's risk pool is financed by the individuals who enroll in it as well as by insurance firms in the state. Under the regulations of the Employee Retirement Income Security Act, administrative-services-only firms need not contribute to risk pools. Although risk pool premiums are high—usually higher than nongroup rates outside of the risk pool—an individual cannot be denied risk pool coverage.

Thus far, total enrollment for all risk pools is only about 20,000 individuals. Preexisting medical conditions are usually excluded for a period of time in order to avoid adverse selection from individuals who are currently undertaking or about to undertake expensive medical treatment (Laudicina and Lipson 1987). The size of the risk pool may vary depending on patient eligibility requirements, the extent of the benefit package, the sources of funding, and the financing mechanism. Risk pools have been criticized as being underfunded, but this is a criticism not of the efficiency of risk pools but rather of society's commitment to risk pools.

There appear to be a number of limitations to risk pools as currently constituted. First, a risk pool is only for high-risk individuals. It is not generally targeted toward low-income individuals or other individuals who may lack health insurance. Second, a risk pool will not attract even the high-risk population if preexisiting conditions are not covered upon inclusion in the pool. Adverse selection may raise the costs of the pools, but this cost has to be weighed against the costs to society of a greater number of uninsured individuals. Third, risk pool arrangements have not been very cost conscious in the payment of providers. A single insurer generally administers each program and pays providers in a fee-for-service manner. A choice of insuring organizations may result in greater cost savings and efficiencies.

The encouragement of the formation of new groups of individuals or the enlargement of existing groups of individuals when risk pools are formed would increase the number of "sponsors" in health care (Enthoven 1988). In the case of risk pools, the sponsors would undoubtedly be state, local, or federal governments. Sponsors would have the flexibility to negotiate price and payment mechanisms with a large number of competing health plans; to reduce information costs to the individuals in the pool by interpreting the provisions of the plans to them; and, of course, to include all high-risk or low-income individuals in their coverage.

Subsidization of insurers

Insuring organizations currently have little incentive to enroll the high-risk, low-income population. One way to encourage insurers to enroll this population is to subsidize them for doing so. The subsidy for enrolling high-risk individuals would have to be equal to the insurer's projected increase in health care costs. An insurer fully reimbursed for the added costs would have no incentive for avoiding high-risk individuals. The subsidy for enrolling low-income individuals might be equal to the projected average per capita health care costs for all enrollees. Subsidized firms could compete on the basis of cost containment rather than through the avoidance of high-risk or low-income individuals. The difficulties in calculating these subsidies may be formidable, however.

Some economists have also suggested subsidies in the form of tax incentives to small employers who offer health insurance to workers below a minimal income level (Wilensky 1988). The program, however, would be difficult to implement since the definitions of "small" employer and "minimal" income level are vague. Further, it is not clear why only small employers should receive such a subsidy. A subsidy would provide small employers with a windfall competitive advantage over large employers.

Expansion of Medicaid

To be eligible for benefits through Medicaid, a state-run program, one must have little or no income and few or no assets. In addition, recipients must be eligible for the Aid to Families with Dependent Children program in the state in which they reside. The income or asset requirement in any state is a function of legislation in that state. If federal law were to lower the eligibility requirements, a greater number of indigent individuals might be included in the Medicaid program. The high-risk, nonpoor population would still lack health insurance, however. Chapter 6 will more fully explore the Medicaid program.

Regulation of Blue Cross and Blue Shield

Since in many states there is substantial regulation of Blue Cross and Blue Shield premiums, open-enrollment periods, and coverage of preexisting conditions, the enrollment of high-risk individuals might be increased by ensuring, through uniform regulation, that Blue Cross and Blue Shield is the insurer of last resort. For example, regulations could mandate that the Blues maintain a continuous, well-advertised, open-enrollment period, with no waiting periods for coverage of preexisting conditions.

The regulation of Blue Cross and Blue Shield might be difficult to enforce, however. For example, if the Blues did not direct the advertising of open-enrollment periods toward high-risk individuals, those individuals would be less likely to be attracted to their plans. Blue Cross and Blue Shield premiums would have to be regulated concurrently since a substantial increase in the health care premium might exclude a large number of individuals.

Incentives would also have to be provided to Blue Cross and Blue Shield to enroll high-risk individuals. Most Blue Cross and Blue Shield plans are exempt from the payment of state premium taxes and most state property taxes. It is unclear if these exemptions are currently equal to the added costs of the enrollment of high-risk individuals or if increased subsidies would be necessary. Regulation of Blue Cross and Blue Shield would also need to be complemented by subsidies to pay for the expected costs of illness for individuals who are indigent.

Expansion of employer-provided health insurance

The government might expand employer-provided health insurance by requiring employers to offer employees a health insurance package that would cover at least a minimal level of care. Since more than three-quarters of all nonagricultural, civilian workers receive their health insurance through their employers, this would be an expansion of the most prevalent structure in the purchase of health insurance. Employers with only a few employees might be exempt from the health insurance requirement since health insurance coverage might constitute a substantial share of the firm's costs. In this latter case, employees might receive their insurance through a state-sponsored risk pool.

Requiring employers to offer health insurance would prevent employers that do not offer health insurance from realizing cost advantages over firms that do. In addition, more private firms would be able to act as informed sponsors of health insurance plans for their employees.

It is unclear who would eventually bear the burden of these increased health care costs. Firms with little competition could shift the increased costs to consumers, in the form of higher prices. If these firms were able to shift costs to consumers, the higher prices would mean that fewer of the firms' goods or services would be purchased. Reduction in demand might lead to higher unemployment and thus an increased number of individuals without health insurance.

In contrast, firms facing substantial competition might have to bear the costs of the health insurance. In this case, the firms might substitute relatively less expensive capital for relatively more expensive labor in order to minimize total costs. Increased unemployment again might result. The extent of this unemployment would depend on the relative size of health insurance premiums as a percentage of the employees' total wage bill. Evidence has suggested, however, that legislated increases in the minimum wage have resulted in higher unemployment rates (Brown 1988).

To reduce the employer's financial burden, the government might mandate that only a specified health benefit package need be offered without a financial commitment by the employer (Wilensky 1988). Under this scheme, the employee would have the benefit of a group sponsor but would, of course, have to bear the full costs of the insurance.

The Uninsured: A Summary

The continuing presence of indigent and high-risk uninsureds is a societal problem that reflects an inequitable distribution of health care resources in the United States. Any attempt to alter the distribution of these resources might involve increased government intervention into the health care system in the form of increased health care benefits, greater government regulation, or both. This greater government intervention might affect the allocation of resources since taxes would have to be raised in some sectors of the economy to pay for the expanded health care benefits. Government regulation also tends to distort the allocation of resources since it generally puts a constraint on a firm's ability to maximize profits or minimize losses. A more equitable distribution of health care resources, however, might be preferred in the belief that health care is a merit good that should be provided in some form regardless of one's health status or ability to pay.

References

Brown, C. (1988). "Minimum Wage Laws: Are They Overrated?" *The Journal of Economic Perspectives* 2 (no. 3): 133–45.

Brown, L. D. (1990). "The Medically Uninsured: Problems, Policies, and Politics," *Journal of Health Politics, Policy, and Law* 15 (no. 2): 413–26.

Eilers, R.D. (1963). *Regulation of Blue Cross and Blue Shield Plans.* Homewood, IL: Richard D. Irwin, Inc.

Employee Benefit Research Institute (1987). *Issue Brief* 66, 10.

Enthoven, A. C. (1988). "Managed Competition of Alternative Delivery Sytems," *Journal of Health Politics, Policy and Law* 13 (no. 2): 305–22.

Fanara, P., Jr., and Greenberg, W. (1985). "The Impact of Competition and Regulation on Blue Cross Enrollment of Non-Group Individuals," *Journal of Risk and Insurance* L11: 185–98.

Farley, P. (1985). "Who are the Uninsured?" *Milbank Quarterly* 63 (no. 3): 476–503.

Feldstein, M. S. (1973). "The Welfare Loss of Excess Health Insurance," *Journal of Political Economy* 81: 251–80.

Feldstein, P. J., Wickizer, T. M., and Wheeler, J. R. C. (1988). "The Effects of Utilization Review Programs on Health Care Use and Expenditures," *New England Journal of Medicine* 318: 310–14.

Frech, H. E., III, and Ginsburg, P. B. (1978). "Competition Among Health Insurers." In *Competition in the Health Care Sector: Past, Present and Future,* ed. W. Greenberg, 167–88. Germantown, MD: Aspen System Corporation.

———. (1988). "Competition among Health Insurers," *Journal of Health Politics, Policy and Law* 13: 279–76.

Goldberg, L., and Greenberg, W. (1977). "The Effects of Physician Controlled Health Insurance: *U.S. vs. Oregon State Medical Society,*" *Journal of Health Politics, Policy and Law* 2: 48–78.

———. (1985). "The Dominant Firm in Health Insurance," *Social Science and Medicine* 20 (no. 7): 720.

———. (1988). "Health Insurance Without Provider Influence: The Limits of Cost Containment," *Journal of Health Politics, Policy and Law* 13: 293–303.

Greenberg, W. (1981). "Provider-Influenced Insurance Plans and Their Impact on Competition: Lessons from Dentistry." In *A New Approach to the Economics of Health Care,* ed. M. Olson, 361–76. Washington DC: American Enterprise Institute.

———. (1989). *Response to AIDS in the Private Sector.* Alexandria, VA: Capitol Publications.

Hadley, J., Steinberg, E. P., and Feder, J. (1990). "Comparison of Uninsured and Privately Insured Hospital Patients," *Journal of American Medical Association* 265 (no. 3): 374–79.

Health Insurance Association of America (1990). *Source Book of Health Insurance Data.* Washington, DC: Health Insurance Association of America.

Johns, L., Anderson, M., and Derzon, R. A. (1985). "Selective Contracting in California: Experience in the Second Year," *Inquiry* 22: 335–47.

Laudicina, S. S., and Lipson, D. J. (1987). *Health Insurance for the Non-Aged Population: The State's Role,* The Intergovernmental Health Policy Project. Washington DC: The George Washington University.

McDonnell, P., Gutenberg, A., Greenberg, L., and Arnott, R. H., III (1986). "Self-Insurer Health Plans," *Health Care Financing Review* 8 (no. 2): 1–15.

Newhouse, J. P. (1988). "Has the Erosion of the Medical Marketplace Ended?" *Journal of Health Politics, Policy and Law* 13: 263–79.

Office of Technology Assessment (1988). *AIDS and Health Insurance, An OTA Survey.* Washington, DC: U.S. Government Printing Office.

Pauly, M. V.(1968). "The Economics of Moral Hazard: Comment," *American Economic Review* 58: 531–37.

Rothschild, M., and Stiglitz, J. (1976). "Equilibrium in Competitive Insurance Markets: An Essay of the Economics of Imperfect Information," *Quarterly Journal of Economics* 90: 629–49.

Swartz, K. (1990). "Why Requiring Employers to Provide Health Insurance Is a Bad Idea," *Journal of Health Politics, Policy and Law* 15 (n. 4): 779–92.

Swartz, K., and McBride, T. D. (1990). "Spells Without Health Insurance: Distributions of Durations and Their Link to Point-in-Time Estimate of the Uninsured," *Inquiry* 27: 281–88.

U.S. Bureau of the Census. (1988). *Statistical Abstract of the United States*, 108th Edition. Washington, DC: U.S. Government Printing Office, Table 749, p. 444.

U.S. Federal Trade Commission (1979). *Medical Participation in Control of Blue Shield and Certain Other Open Panel Medical Prepayment Plans*, 59. Washington DC: U.S. Government Printing Office.

Wilensky, G. R. (1988). "Filling the Gaps In Health Insurance: Impact on Competition," *Health Affairs* 7: 133–49.

5

Alternative Delivery Systems

Blue Cross and Blue Shield, commercial carriers, and third party administrators are components of the private insurance industry that arose primarily to improve access to the traditional, fee-for-service health care delivery system. The private insurance industry has also given rise to alternatives to that system. Health maintenance organizations and preferred provider organizations—alternative delivery systems—are the subject of this chapter.

A health maintenance organization is basically a prepaid health insurance plan in which an organization accepts contractual responsibility for the delivery of a stated range of health services to an enrolled population. A preferred provider organization is an organization that contracts with a subset of providers in an attempt to achieve lower costs or to achieve higher quality care. PPO enrollees pay a premium and receive care from this subset of providers, or they may choose to pay additional fees and select other providers, who are generally not under cost constraints.

In 1988, HMOs and PPOs accounted for approximately one-third of all individuals who had private health insurance coverage (Health Insurance Association of America 1990). Enrollment in HMOs grew from 9.1 million individuals in 1980 to 32.4 million individuals in 1989 (Health Insurance Association of America 1990; Office of HMOs 1980). Enrollment in PPOs was virtually zero in 1980 and approximately 36 million individuals in 1988 (Health Insurance Association of America 1990). Of the total enrollment in HMOs, there are approximately 1 million persons whose premiums are paid by Medicare and more than 800,000 whose premiums are paid by Medicaid (InterStudy 1987, 1988).

Health Maintenance Organizations

There are four models for health maintenance organizations: staff, group, network, and individual practice association (IPA). The staff-model HMO provides services through its own physicians, who are paid employees of the HMO. The group-model HMO contracts with an independent medical group or a partnership or corporation of licensed health professionals for the provision of health services. The network-model HMO contracts with two or more group practices; physicians who work for the HMO may receive payment on a fee-for-service, salary, or capitation basis. The IPA, often sponsored by local, county, or state medical societies (sometimes in reaction to an increasing market share of HMOs not sponsored by physicians), contracts with physicians to deliver services from their individual offices (Goldberg and Greenberg 1980; Welch, Hillman, and Pauly 1990). Physicians are usually paid on a fee-for-service basis, but some form of peer review exists.

Physicians participating in staff, group, and most network HMOs are usually at risk for health care costs that exceed their revenues. Physicians are also at risk in an increasing number of IPAs (Welch 1987). Physicians, therefore, have no incentive to perform tests or initiate hospital admissions that may be deemed unnecessary. Moreover, an HMO itself has incentives to avoid duplication of services, to use lower-cost medical personnel, and to use less expensive outpatient services. The organization that is not vigilant in these areas loses market share to its competitors.

More than two-thirds of HMOs are for-profit enterprises (InterStudy 1988, 107). There has also been substantial entry into the marketplace by Blue Cross and Blue Shield plans, commercial insurers, and corporate firms, which have purchased and started a number of HMOs. The Blues have sponsored 96 HMOs, with enrollments totalling 4.5 million people (InterStudy 1988a, 15). At the beginning of 1988 there were 320 national HMOs, with a total enrollment of 18 million individuals (Blue Cross and Blue Shield Association 1988, 2). (A national HMO belongs to an organization that owns or operates separate HMOs in two or more states.) The large number of HMOs owned by HMO chains may be due to economies of scale in the marketing and administration of these chains as well as to an increased number of acquisitions of HMOs whose assets were believed to be undervalued in the marketplace (Gruber, Shadle, and Polich 1988, 205).

Growth and federal qualification

There are a number of reasons why HMOs have grown so rapidly over the last decade. Rising health care costs themselves may have stimulated growth as an alternative to traditional fee-for-service insurance arrangements. This is not unlike the phenomenon that economist Joseph Schumpeter (1942) attributed to many industries when he observed new, innovative firms entering to compete with more costly, existing firms. HMOs have grown most rapidly in areas with very mobile populations. As individuals have moved to new geographic areas, without attachments to local physicians, they have been attracted to HMOs that could provide them with or refer them to family physicians as well as physician specialists (Goldberg and Greenberg 1981). Finally, both a decrease in organized resistance by the medical profession and an increase in antitrust activity by the government (see Chapter 8) have made it easier for HMOs to grow.

The federal government legitimized the creation of HMOs with the passage of the HMO Act of 1973 (PL 93–222). Under this Act, an HMO was required to have an open-enrollment period at least once a year. Community rating was also required, which means that an HMO must divide its total costs (and premiums) evenly among all members regardless of the costs of any individual group. This provision increases the premium the HMO must charge to groups experiencing lower-than-average risks and makes it more difficult for the HMO to compete with other health insurance plans.

The Act set forth criteria to be met by any HMO desiring federal qualification. Federally qualified HMOs, for instance, must offer a specific minimum benefit package. All members must pay for these services, regardless of whether all or most consumers would want the services. In addition to physician and inpatient hospital services, for example, short-term mental health services, preventive dental care for children, and diagnostic and therapeutic radiological services must be offered. The Act did, however, require employers with 25 or more employees, located in an area with a federally qualified HMO, to offer their employees the HMO option in addition to any traditional health benefit plans. Moreover, the Act made available to qualified HMOs $50,000 feasibility grants, $125,000 planning grants, and development funds of up to $1 million. Currently, more than half of all HMOs are federally qualified (InterStudy 1988a, 10).

The 1973 Act has been amended a number of times. A 1976 provision (PL 94–460) limits the open-enrollment requirement to HMOs that are at least five years old or have at least 50,000 enrollees and that do not have a federal deficit. The HMO Act Amendments of 1988 (PL 100–517) reduce some of the requirements on employers who might offer HMOs. For example, employers do not have to contribute equally toward the premiums of HMOs and fee-for-service plans. In fact, by 1995, most employers will no longer be required to offer HMOs.

How do HMOs compete?

Health maintenance organizations may compete among themselves and with other fee-for-service and alternative delivery system plans in a number of ways. Convenience of location and reduced waiting times may be nonprice modes of competition. A well-established corporate name, such as Blue Cross or Kaiser, may also be a factor in competition.

HMOs compete to avoid high-risk individuals in the same way that traditional insurers may. This is especially true in the market for individuals who do not enroll as members of groups. For example, HMOs and traditional insurers have attempted to avoid individual applicants who have AIDS or who have been infected with the AIDS virus (Greenberg 1989). HMOs do well in attracting younger couples with children—desirable enrollees—because HMOs usually eliminate the transaction costs of paying the deductibles and copayments characteristic of most traditional insurance plans. HMO benefit packages may also include well-baby care as an attraction to younger couples. The usual necessity of severing the relationship with one's fee-for-service physician upon enrollment in an HMO tends to screen out high-risk individuals; the patients most likely to give up their doctor are those in better health (Goldberg and Greenberg 1981).

On the other hand, some acutely ill patients will be attracted to HMOs because of the minimal copayments and deductibles (or the absence of copayments or deductibles). HMO benefit packages may also be more comprehensive than commercial insurance arrangements of similar cost, which would attract higher-risk patients to HMOs. Most evidence to date suggests that the case mix of HMO enrollees is not much different than that in fee-for-service plans (Luft 1981).

HMOs may also compete on the size of the premiums they charge individuals and employer groups. Yearly premiums of HMOs, especially staff-model HMOs, are less than those charged by fee-for-service plans since staff-model HMOs have generally experienced lower costs (Luft 1981).

HMOs may attempt to compete on the basis of quality of care. The preventive services provided by many HMOs may enhance quality of care for members, as may HMOs' reluctance to perform duplicative services or to foster unnecessary hospital admissions or surgery. Quality of care is difficult to define; Luft (1981), however, found little difference in quality of care between HMOs and fee-for-service plans. However, Luft (1988) acknowledges that most studies have been based on data from only a few of the most established HMOs.

Since an important difference between HMOs and the fee-for-service sector has been the significantly lower costs of HMOs, it is of interest whether the lower costs of HMOs can be translated into lower costs in the fee-for-service sector in the same way that lower-cost and lower-priced firms elsewhere in the economy can stimulate their competitors to reduce costs. For example, when lower-priced supermarkets entered the retail food industry, existing small grocery stores had to cut their prices or go out of business (Adelman 1959). It appears that HMOs can have a competitive effect on the fee-for-service sector, but the precise nature of this effect and its magnitude are unclear.

One study showed that the greater the penetration of HMOs into a marketplace, the lower the hospital utilization and the more comprehensive the benefit package of the competing Blue Cross plans. That is, Blue Cross appeared to be focusing on two central HMO characteristics to maintain or increase its share of the health insurance market (Goldberg and Greenberg 1980). In contrast, McLaughlin (1988) has shown that physicians and hospitals do not reduce their prices when confronted with HMO competition but rather increase their advertising or engage in nonprice rivalry. Still other studies have shown that competition with HMOs has resulted in decreased hospital utilization by Blue Cross in specific geographic areas, such as Northern California and Hawaii (Goldberg and Greenberg 1979).

Luft (1978) found that HMOs have lower costs per capita than do fee-for-service plans. In particular, previous studies have shown that prepaid group practices in which physicians were at risk had significantly lower costs, while IPAs in which physicians were not at risk had costs about the same as the fee-for-service sector. Most HMO savings have occurred because, compared to individuals in fee-for-service plans, members of HMOs have had fewer admissions to hospitals (Luft 1978). Once patients are admitted to the hospital, however, their lengths of stay appear to be the same for HMOs and fee-for-service plans (Luft 1978).

Although HMOs have had lower costs than the fee-for-service sector in any given year, the increase in costs over time of HMOs and fee-for-service plans has been about the same (Newhouse, Schwartz, Williams, and Witsberger 1985). This same relative increase in costs is a distressing conclusion for those who believe that enrolling more people in HMOs can slow the rise in health care costs. If HMOs do have lower costs than fee-for-service plans, it appears that, at best, one might expect increased enrollment to produce an initial decline in health care costs. After an initial decline, however, costs would rise as fast as they do under fee-for-service plans. The reason for this increase in HMO costs over time is that, while HMOs may be more efficient, they are subject to the same legal and professional pressures as fee-for-service plans in their diagnosis and treatment of patients and in their use of the latest innovations in health care technology (see Chapter 10).

Preferred Provider Organizations

Preferred provider organizations may be sponsored by Blue Cross and Blue Shield, commercial insurers, corporate firms, or even physicians and hospitals. Physicians or hospitals or both physicians and hospitals may themselves be preferred providers. Physicians who are members of PPOs may have to agree to utilization review and reduced fee schedules. In return, such physicians may realize higher market shares as they are promoted by the organization. Organizations may advertise the names and locations of these preferred physicians in addition to requiring little or no copayment of patients who patronize them. A hospital that is a member of a PPO may also be advertised more heavily in return for increased discounts on its charges to the organization.

Financial risk is usually assumed by the organization rather than by the providers. Unlike the staff-model or group-model HMO, in nearly all PPO arrangements the physician providers still practice fee-for-service medicine. PPO physicians generally practice in their own offices; staff-model HMO physicians usually practice at facilities owned by the organization. Hence, the financial investment necessary to begin a PPO is minimal, and barriers to entry are modest.

PPOs explicitly inject more information and bargaining power into the market for health services. They provide information to potential subscribers by publicizing the relative prices charged by preferred and nonpreferred providers. By their bargaining power, they are able to negotiate with providers for reduced prices and increased utilization review. A PPO is able to set provider prices based on its knowledge of the prices charged by its array of providers in particular geographic areas. The organization should also have data on the costs of performing certain procedures. In this way it can monitor the behavior and set the fees of providers.

Moreover, the bargaining power of insuring organizations is especially pronounced in preferred provider organizations. Because of its ability to direct a large number of patients toward particular providers, a PPO is likely to obtain discounts and practice an economical form of medicine. This is not to suggest that PPOs offer inferior care. There are a large number of PPOs in the marketplace, each with a different emphasis on quality and price.

Preferred provider organizations were first begun after the 1979 Federal Trade Commission decision against the American Medical Association, 94 FTC 701 (1979). In that decision, affirmed by the Supreme Court, the FTC ruled that the AMA Code of Ethics, which required that all area physicians be reimbursed at the same schedule of prices by health insurance plans, was in restraint of trade (Weller 1984, 1351). The Code of Ethics prohibited, in effect, groups of physicians from competing with one another economically. Differential reimbursement would increase competition among physicians since existing lower-priced physicians might accept lower payments than their more expensive colleagues. Under the guidelines of the AMA's Code of Ethics, competition among physicians would be based on nonprice factors alone (Weller 1984, 1357).

Preferred provider organizations may increase competition in both the provider marketplace and the insurer marketplace (Gabel and Ermann 1985). Providers will compete among themselves to be offered by PPOs. Once selected as "preferred," providers will compete against those providers who have elected not to change their behavior or fees. The addition of a PPO creates competition in the insurer marketplace by expanding consumer choice. When PPOs realize cost savings, they also put downward pressure on the premiums of other insuring organizations (Dranove, Satterwhite, and Sindelar 1986). At the very least, preferred provider organizations provide an alternative to traditional fee-for-service and health maintenance organization plans.

Although the enrollment in PPOs has grown steadily, the decision in a landmark antitrust case, *Arizona v. Maricopa County Medical Society*, 457 US 332 (1982), may have hampered the increase. In that case, a physician-sponsored PPO, the Maricopa Medical Foundation, was found guilty of restraint of trade and price fixing for signing 70 percent of the physicians in Maricopa County in a preferred provider organization. This PPO attempted to contain costs by setting maximum fees and instituting utilization review. The Supreme Court ruled, ironically, that the large market share of the Maricopa Medical Foundation, its control by physicians, and its maximum-fee provision reduced the competition in the marketplace. Because of this decision, providers may be reluctant to sponsor their own PPOs.

At the end of 1987 there were 646 operational or preoperational PPOs. Each state had at least one PPO, while California had 110 PPOs (American Medical Care and Review Association 1987). Why the large number of PPOs? The first reason may be the Supreme Court decision in the Federal Trade Commission's case against the American Medical Association. The second reason may be the increase in health care costs, in the same way that increases in health care costs have stimulated the growth of HMOs. The third reason may be the gradual elimination of state laws restricting the formation of preferred provider organizations or competition among groups of physicians (Rolph, Ginsburg, and Hosek 1987). Finally, providers have been more amenable to joining PPOs or to forming organizations themselves as the physician population has increased and as the percentage of empty beds in hospitals has increased.

References

Adelman, M. A. (1959). *A&P: A Study in Price-Cost Behavior and Public Policy.* Cambridge, MA: Harvard University Press.

American Medical Care and Review Association (1987). *Directory of Preferred Provider Organizations and the Industry Report on PPO Development.* Bethesda, MD: The Association.

Blue Cross and Blue Shield Association (1988). *The Blue Cross and Blue Shield Organization,* 2. Chicago: The Association.

Dranove, D., Satterwhite, M., and Sindelar, J. (1986). "The Effect of Injecting Price Competition into the Hospital Market: The Case of Preferred Provider Organizations," *Inquiry* 23: 419–31.

Federal Trade Commission v. American Medical Association, 94 FTC 701 (1979).

Gabel, J., and Ermann, D. (1985). "Preferred Provider Organizations: Performance, Problems, and Promise," *Health Affairs* 4: 24–39.

Goldberg, L. G., and Greenberg, W. (1979). "Competitive Response to Blue Cross and Blue Shield to the Health Maintenance Organization in Northern California and Hawaii," *Medical Care* 16: 1019–28.

———. (1980). "The Competitive Response of Blue Cross to the Health Maintenance Organization," *Economic Inquiry* 17: 55–68.

———. (1981). "The Determinants of HMO Enrollment and Growth," *Health Services Research* 18: 421–38.

Greenberg, W. (1989). *Response to AIDS in the Private Sector.* Alexandria, VA: Capitol Publications.

Gruber, L. R., Shadle, M., and Polich, C. L. (1988). "From Movement to Industry: The Growth of HMOs," *Health Affairs* 7: 197–208.

Health Insurance Association of America (1990). *Source Book of Health Insurance Data,* 7, 21, 31. Washington, DC: Health Insurance Association of America.

InterStudy (1987). *Medicaid and HMO Data Book.* Excelsior, MN: InterStudy.

———. (1988a). *The InterStudy Edge.* Excelsior, MN: InterStudy.

———. (1988b). *Update of Medicare HMOs.* Excelsior, MN: InterStudy.

Luft, H. S. (1978). "How do Health Maintenance Organizations Achieve Their Savings?" *The New England Journal of Medicine* 298: 1336–43.

———. (1981). *Performance.* New York: John Wiley.

———. (1988). "HMOs and the Quality of Care," *Inquiry* 25: 147–56.

McLaughlin, C. G. (1988). "Market Response to HMOs: Price Competition or Rivalry?" *Inquiry* 25: 207–18.

Newhouse, J. P., Schwartz, W. B., Williams, A. P., and Witsberger, C. (1985). "Are Fee-for-Service Costs Increasing Faster than HMO Costs?" *Medical Care* 23: 960–66.

Office of HMOs (1980). *National HMO Census.* Washington, DC: U.S. Government Printing Office.

Rolph, E. S., Ginsburg, P. B., and Hosek, S. D. (1987). "The Regulation of Preferred Provider Arrangements," *Health Affairs* 6: 32–45.

Schumpeter, J. A. (1942). *Capitalism, Socialism, and Democracy.* New York: Harper & Row.

Welch, W. P. (1987). "The New Structure of Individual Practice Associations," *Journal of Health Politics, Policy and Law* 12: 723–39.

Welch, W. P., Hillman, A. L., and Pauly, M. V. (1990). "Toward New Typologies for HMOs," *The Milbank Quarterly* 68 (no. 2): 221–43.

Weller, C. D. (1984). "'Free Choice' as a Restraint of Trade in American Health Care Delivery and Insurance," *Iowa Law Review* 69: 1351–94.

6

Health Insurance in the Public Sector

Medicare and Medicaid were enacted in 1965 to help the elderly, the disabled, and the indigent pay for health care services. The elderly and the disabled were usually not members of employer groups, they were at high risk for illness relative to the rest of the population, and they generally lacked the financial resources to purchase health insurance. The indigent by and large were not members of employer groups and lacked the resources to pay for health care insurance on their own.

In Chapter 4 it was suggested that insurance firms in the private sector have little incentive to insure the elderly, the disabled, and the indigent. It was also suggested that health care is a merit good that many would suggest should be available in some measure to all citizens. This chapter will examine whether the Medicare and Medicaid programs are the most efficient schemes of insuring the elderly, the disabled, and the indigent; whether the programs are financed efficiently; and, finally, whether these programs have provided their target populations sufficient access to health care.

Medicare

Medicare provided coverage for more than 33 million beneficiaries in 1988 (Prospective Payment Assessment Commission 1990a, 95). Individuals over the age of 65, individuals who have been disabled for more than 24 consecutive months, and individuals who have end-stage renal disease are entitled to Medicare regardless of their income or the size of their asset holdings.

Part A of Medicare provides inpatient hospital care, intensive care, and services in skilled nursing facilities for up to 150 days a year. In addition, Medicare pays for hospice services and for home health services for individuals who must stay at home. Part B of the Medicare program provides physician services and outpatient hospital care. Private insurance carriers such as Blue Cross and Blue Shield may act as fiscal intermediaries in the administration and payment of covered Medicare services.

Medicare does not pay the complete cost for each of these services; patients must meet deductible, copayment, and eligibility requirements. Consequently, many individuals elect to purchase "Medigap" insurance from Blue Cross and Blue Shield and commercial carriers in the private sector to help pay for health care expenses. Only 23 percent of Medicare enrollees do not have at least some supplemental insurance coverage (Prospective Payment Assessment Commission 1990a, 99).

Enrollment and expenditures of the Medicare program

In 1966, Medicare's first year of operation, there were approximately 19 million Medicare beneficiaries (Health Care Financing Administration 1987, 13). By 1980, there were approximately 28 million beneficiaries. Expenditures for 1966, for a half-year of operation (Medicare began to pay for health care services on July 1, 1966), were $1.019 billion (Health Care Financing Administration 1986, 20). By 1980, expenditures exceeded $36 billion; at the end of 1988, Medicare expenditures were $88.5 billion (Prospective Payment Assessment Commission 1990a, 96).

Of total Medicare expenditures, Part B expenditures have increased faster than Part A expenditures. In 1966 Part B expenditures accounted for approximately 13 percent of Medicare payments, and in 1988 Part B expenditures accounted for approximately 40 percent of Medicare payments (Prospective Payment Assessment Commission 1990a, 96).

The financing of Medicare

Although a public program, Medicare is not financed primarily by general funds. Rather, Part A is mostly financed by a payroll tax, while Part B is financed by premiums paid by beneficiaries as well as by federal government general funds. The Part A financing structure is regressive. That is, wealthier individuals pay a lesser percentage of their income to the hospital insurance trust fund than do poorer individuals. In 1988, for example, employed individuals paid 7.51 percent of their gross income up to $45,000 to the fund. An individual, therefore, who had an income of $45,000 would pay $3,380 into the fund or 7.51 percent of his or her income. In contrast, an individual who had an income of $100,000 would also pay $3,380 into the fund or 3.38 percent of his or her income (U.S. Congress 1990, 161).

Part B financing is also regressive. If the Part B option is chosen (and more than 90 percent of Medicare enrollees choose it), the same monthly premium is paid regardless of income. In 1990, the monthly premium was $31.90 (Prospective Payment Assessment Commission 1990b, 97).

Medicare as catastrophic health insurance

Medicare does not pay for catastrophic health expenses. Rather, after an initial deductible—$540 in 1988, for example (equal to the average cost of a day in the hospital)—Medicare would pay all hospital expenses for the next 60 days (Prospective Payment Assessment Commission 1990a, 79). However, after 60 days Medicare required a copayment of one-quarter of the deductible per day until the 90th day. For the next 60 days Medicare required a copayment of half of the deductible. After 150 days, the beneficiary was required to pay the hospital's full charge.

In addition, a lifetime reserve of 60 days could be used to supplement the daily coverage. However, on each admission to the hospital during the year, the pattern of deductibles and copayments would start again. In 1985, for example, there were 6,036 beneficiaries who used up their covered and partially covered days and were left, therefore, without any Medicare insurance coverage for that year (Sobaski 1989).

Clearly, Medicare was not designed to insure for catastrophic health problems that would necessitate long stays in the hospital. Under the original Medicare provisions, beneficiaries paid an increasing share of the hospital costs during an extended hospital stay. During the later stages of an illness, when patients tend to need hospital insurance most, Medicare paid a smaller and smaller share of the hospital bill.

Medicare as an entitlement program

Each individual who meets the eligibility requirements for Medicare receives the full amount of Medicare benefits. There is no adjustment to the amount of benefits based on one's income. High-income individuals, who might be able to afford expenses for hospital and physician visits, receive the same benefits as low-income individuals. Moreover, the people who are covered by Medicare are the oldest people in U.S. society.

One might question the equity of providing Medicare coverage to the most affluent individuals in this oldest age group, when such a large number of younger, poorer individuals do not have health insurance. Although both high- and low-income individuals may have paid taxes into the program, the program need not entitle everyone to the same benefits. Taxes are frequently used for programs that provide unequal benefits to various individuals and no benefits at all to others. For example, people throughout the United States may pay taxes that are earmarked to improve national parks on the West Coast, parks many of the people may never enter. Individuals also pay taxes for welfare benefits they may never receive or defense expenditures they oppose.

Medicare and cost containment—hospitals

Until the diagnostic-related group payment system was implemented in October 1983, the federal entitlement programs reimbursed hospitals retrospectively for all reasonable costs. Mandatory prospective reimbursement programs had already been introduced in nine states, while New Jersey had even established its own DRG system in 1980 that included reimbursement by all third-party payers.

With the DRG payment system, the Health Care Financing Administration (the administrative agency of the Department of Health and Human Services) changed from a passive payer of the costs incurred by each hospital to an active controller of hospital costs. For the first time since the inception of the Medicare program, HCFA would pay a component of the health care sector on a prospective rather than a retrospective basis. Psychiatric, long-term care, children's, and rehabilitation institutions, however, are excluded from DRGs.

The DRG system is a method for classifying the output of a hospital by certain diagnostic and therapeutic attributes peculiar to each patient. Each of the 490 DRGs stems from a principal diagnosis, an operating-room procedure, a secondary diagnosis, the patient's age, discharge status, or a combination of these variables. DRG 89, for instance, identifies inpatient hospital procedures appropriate for patients with pneumonia and pleurisy; DRG 127 is heart failure and shock; DRG 138 is cardiac arrhythmia and conduction disorders; DRG 140 is angina pectoris; and DRG 296 is nutritional and miscellaneous metabolic disorders. Two DRGs (469 and 470) are for diagnoses that are invalid or not easily classified (Prospective Payment Assessment Commission 1991).

Currently, the amount of payment under DRGs is adjusted and calculated separately for the geographic location (urban or rural) of hospitals, for differences in wages paid, for teaching and nonteaching hospitals, for percentage of low-income patients, and for very extensive or very expensive hospital stays. Adjustments are also made for hospitals that are the communities' sole providers of hospital care, for national and regional referral centers, and for Medicare-dependent hospitals (U.S. Congress 1990, 302–78). The DRG payment mechanism will recognize and pay for day ("extraordinarily" long hospital stays) and cost ("very-high costs relative to the average") outliers, although outliers are set such that they only account for about 5 or 6 percent of total DRG payments to hospitals (U.S. Congress 1988, 63–67).

The DRGs attempt to take into consideration the case mix of hospitals in order to prevent hospitals with patients with more severe illnesses from realizing lower net incomes regardless of efficiency considerations. Horn et al. (1985) suggest that teaching hospitals, for example, may have a greater proportion of patients who are severely ill than other hospitals.

Direct medical education and bad debts incurred by Medicare patients are reimbursed retrospectively because they have little to do with inpatient operating costs. Capital expenditures, which include depreciation and interest for new beds, new equipment, and new renovations as well as a return on equity for the for-profit hospitals, are also not included in the DRG prospective payment since hospitals vary significantly in the procurement and depreciation of their capital. If hospitals were reimbursed prospectively for capital expenditures, such as a fixed amount for each Medicare admission, there is concern that gains or losses from the reimbursement might provide windfall gains to hospitals that had just completed major capital expansions and windfall losses to hospitals that were about to begin expansions. In addition, there is concern that prospective capital payments will curtail new technology.

The incentives of the DRG system

Since the DRG system provides a fixed payment for each episode of illness, the incentives for the hospital are quite different than under traditional cost-plus reimbursement, which reimbursed hospitals for all costs incurred. Hospitals under DRGs, for example, have incentives to perform fewer services and reduce inefficiencies in order to realize greater income (or prevent losses). Further, DRGs may create incentives to increase the number of patients, since economies of scale in treatment may result in lower costs.

Hospitals have incentives to increase the number of admissions per patient since each time an individual is admitted the DRG calculation begins again. Hospitals also have incentives to perform procedures (and raise prices) on an outpatient basis, since these procedures are not covered by DRGs. Since there are only 490 DRGs, and many individuals have multiple diagnoses, there are incentives to code the discharged patient with the most remunerative among the potential DRG categories. Moreover, the hospital may also have incentives to unbundle services rendered to patients with multiple diagnoses and to treat each diagnosis as yet another admission. In addition, hospitals may attempt to raise prices and recoup some of their costs in the private sector, where commercial carriers and Blue Cross and Blue Shield may have relatively less-elastic demand curves.

Recognizing the incentives created by the DRG payment system, the Department of Health and Human Services incorporated in the system a peer review organization (PRO) component to monitor hospital use, especially hospital admission procedures, and quality of care. PROs also monitor the coding of DRGs and claims made for covered services. Hospitals receiving Medicare reimbursement are required to contract with the designated PRO in their area. Moreover, a single "Super PRO" was established to oversee all PRO activities.

Most important, DRG rates are administered prices set by the government rather than competitive prices set by the marketplace (Noll and Enthoven 1984). Rather than the seller determining the price at which the good or service can be sold, as is true in any other industry, the government (buyer) sets and pays the DRG rates. In any other industry, prices are established by competitive forces among the firms as well as by the potential demand of the buyers. To establish its price, the individual firm must be able to estimate its marginal and average cost curves as well as the demand curve for its good or service. If the price is set too high, the firm may lose market share or even go out of business. In most industries, one finds an array of prices that reflects the cost and quality of and the demand for the good or service sold.

In contrast, the government sets DRG prices based on the average costs of all hospitals for each DRG. In the hospital industry, therefore, a single administered price will prevent an efficient hospital from securing an increased market share by charging a lower price. It will also prevent a superior quality hospital from charging a higher price.

Hospitals may experience increased profits or losses if their costs are below or above the administered DRG price. Hospitals that are most efficient in treating patients with particular DRGs may choose to specialize in those DRGs only. Hospitals that are inefficient in treating patients with particular DRGs will have incentives to discontinue services for those DRGs. This specialization of services may promote more efficiency in the hospital system. Hospitals that are less efficient in some DRG services must become more efficient in others or face closure.

How effective have DRGs been?

Although the DRG payment system created incentives for increases in hospital admissions, the number of admissions has thus far decreased. This decrease could be a continuation of a long-term trend over the last decade or the effect of the PROs, the cost-containment efforts of other third-party payers, or other unknown causes. Table 6.1 shows Medicare discharges from hospitals prior to and since the implementation of DRGs. Sloan, Morrisey, and Valvona (1988) suggest that the greatest savings of the DRG program are due to the reduction in hospital admissions (or discharges) per capita. Length of stay in short-term acute care hospitals has also been reduced. Newhouse and Byne (1988) have suggested that some patients may have been shifted to DRG-exempt

Table 6.1 Medicare Discharges per 1,000 Enrollees, 1972–1986

Year	*Discharges per 1,000 Enrollees*
1972	302
1975	325
1980	366
1982	382
1983	387
1984	363
1985	328
1986	322

Source: Helling, C., and Keene, R. (1989). "Use and Cost of Short-Stay Hospital Inpatient Services under Medicare, 1986," *Health Care Financing Review* 10 (no. 4): 95.

hospitals, such as rehabilitative, psychiatric, long-term care, and pediatric hospitals, which have experienced increased lengths of stays since the implementation of DRGs.

Expenditures for inpatient hospitalization per capita for Medicare beneficiaries have increased since the DRG system was implemented, but not as rapidly as Medicare outpatient expenditures (Table 6.2). These data are consistent with the hypothesis that expenditures will grow at a greater pace in the portion of the health care sector over which the DRG system does not exercise constraint.

Economic theory would suggest that hospitals would be able to shift costs from the Medicare payer to other third-party payers depending on the elasticity of demand of the other third party payers. If other third parties were also aggressive in cost containment, it would be less probable that costs could be shifted to them. Moreover, if the hospital finds it too costly to separate its cost-cutting measures for Medicare patients from the remainder of its patients, costs are less likely to be shifted. Thus far, the evidence suggests that hospital costs have not been shifted to other payers (Sloan, Morrisey, and Valvona 1988, 217). It is very difficult to measure the effects of DRGs on the quality of care, especially in so short a time frame. However, Sloan, Morrisey, and Valvona (1988, 215) have tentatively concluded that inpatients

Table 6.2 Inpatient and Outpatient Medicare Expenditures per Enrollee, 1983–1988

Year	*Hospital Inpatient Expenditures (in billions)*	*Hospital Outpatient Expenditures (in billions)*	*Enrollees (in millions)*	*Inpatient Expenditures per Enrollee*	*Outpatient Expenditures per Enrollee*
1983	$37.4	$3.3	30.0	$1,246	$110
1984	41.6	3.8	30.4	1,368	125
1985	44.1	4.4	31.1	1,418	141
1986	45.8	5.3	31.8	1,440	167
1987	47.3	6.2	32.4	1,460	191
1988	49.9	7.0	33.0	1,512	212

Sources: Prospective Payment Assessment Commission (1990). *Medicare Prospective Payment and the American Health Care System, Report to Congress,* Washington, DC: U.S. Government Printing Office, Table 4–7, p. 96.

Committee on Ways and Means (1990). *Overview of Entitlement Programs; Background Material and Data on Programs Within the Jurisdiction of the Committee on Ways and Means,* Washington, DC: U.S. Government Printing Office, Table 25, p. 169.

have not been "denied beneficial care" because of the Medicare DRG system.

It is possible that the increase in the number of hospital closings is due to the DRG payment system. Eighty-one hospitals closed in the United States in 1988 (*Modern Healthcare* 1989). Since many of these hospitals were rural hospitals, it is possible that the lower DRG rate paid to the rural hospitals may not be adequate reimbursement for care for a population that is apt to be uninsured and to have a higher poverty rate. The closings could also be due to the diseconomies of scale experienced by many of the smaller hospitals. These smaller hospitals may be the inefficient firms in the hospital industry and, like inefficient firms in other industries, have little choice but to merge or go out of business. If the smaller hospitals are inefficient firms, it is probably more efficient from society's view for them to vacate the industry.

Medicare and cost containment—physician services

For fee-for-service treatment, the Medicare program has paid physicians on the basis of historical costs. Physician fees were determined by comparing the fees a physician charged for particular procedures with the fees the physician customarily charged in the past year and the fees peer physicians were charging for the same procedure in the same geographic area. Medicare would pay the lesser of the customary fee (the fee charged by the physician) or the 75th percentile of the prevailing fee (the fee charged by peer physicians in the same geographic area) for the same procedure. This lesser amount is called the "reasonable" fee.

Under this fee schedule, historical charges by physicians would be the prime ingredient of future fees. Physicians could elect to accept assignment—that is, accept what Medicare deemed the reasonable fee—and be reimbursed directly by Medicare. Alternatively, physicians, on a case-by-case basis, could charge an amount greater than that reasonable fee and collect the entire fee from the patient directly.

This system of charges based on historical fees has been criticized because the fees physicians charge may not be equal to the marginal or incremental cost of providing the service (Hsiao, Braun, Yntema, and Becker 1988). This may be due to disparate insurance coverage for different physician visits and procedures. For example, in the private sector, physicians such as surgeons, radiologists, anesthesiologists, and pathologists, who primarily perform their services in hospitals have generally been well insured. Demand for their services from the insured individual has been relatively inelastic. In general, patients also see these physicians much less frequently and would have a much more difficult time in comparing fees.

Economists have suggested revisions in physician fees to reflect more accurately the resources included in the service (Hsiao, Braun, Yntema, and Becker 1988). Hsiao, Braun, Yntema, and Becker (1988) maintain that physicians, such as internists, who spend larger amounts of time with patients, may be underpaid relative to surgeons, who may spend less time performing the service. In their resource-based relative value scale (RBRVS), Hsiao et al. would include only the costs of performing a service.

The costs of physician services might include the total work input performed by the physician for each service, including the amount and intensity of the time, the overhead costs of running a practice, and the costs of professional liability insurance. The fees would also be adjusted according to the geographic area in which the physician practices. Physicians would be paid, based on these criteria, regardless of the quality or performance of a particular physician. In 1992, Medicare will begin paying physicians based on this schedule.

An alteration in physician fees, however, may not control the number of services performed or the involvement of more than one physician treating a particular procedure. Gabel and Rice (1985) have suggested, for example, that the number of services may increase if fees or prices are held constant. Moreover, the RBRVS only seems to examine the supply side of the market. It is not sensitive to fluctuations in demand, which has an equal role in the determination of fees. All factors held constant, an increase in demand for pediatricians because of an increase in the number of children, for example, should increase fees for these physicians.

To contain total Medicare expenditures for physician services, annual updates of the fee schedule will be contingent on the calculation of volume performance standards, or growth in total Medicare expenditures for physician services. If total Medicare expenditures for physician services exceed a target set by the government, physician fees will be reduced in the subsequent year.

Because volume performance standards include expenditures for all physicians, those physicians who practice conservative medicine will realize reductions in fees equal to those who may be more profligate in their use of tests and procedures. Indeed, perverse incentives are created for each individual physician to perform more procedures for fear of receiving less income the subsequent year.

Medicare, HMOs, and competitive medical plans

Because of the difficulties in containing Medicare expenditures for hospital and physician care under a fee-for-service arrangement, the federal government has allowed Medicare beneficiaries to enroll in alternative delivery systems. In addition to making costs more manageable, alternative delivery systems may provide competition to the fee-for-service sector and expand consumer choice in the same way that choice may be provided in the private sector. Beneficiaries may enroll in federally qualified health maintenance organizations as well as in competitive medical plans (CMPs). Unlike federally qualified HMOs, CMPs can experience-rate their enrollees. More than one-half of the enrollees of the alternative delivery system must be from the private sector, and each system must have a total of at least 5,000 enrollees (Merlis 1988, 11–12).

Currently, there are nearly 1 million Medicare beneficiaries enrolled in 110 HMOs and 23 CMPs (Rossiter and Langwell 1988, 124). All of these organizations provide at least physician and inpatient care, diagnostic tests, and preventive and emergency services. The alternative delivery systems are allowed to charge a premium or impose deductibles or copayments and are at risk for expenses that exceed income. For each enrolled beneficiary, the organization receives a fixed payment equal to 95 percent of the adjusted average per capita cost (AAPCC) of Medicare beneficiaries in the local area, adjusted by case-mix measures such as age and sex. There is some question about whether the AAPCC is the most accurate reflection of health care costs in a particular area. Critics have asserted, for example, that it may simply perpetuate existing inefficiencies in particular areas (Anderson, Steinberg, Holloway, and Cantor 1986).

Thus far, in some selected demonstration areas, both HMOs and CMPs have realized hospitalization rates of only about half of fee-for-service hospital days. This comparison, however, is not adjusted for higher-risk beneficiaries who may have elected to remain in the fee-for-service system (Rossiter, Nelson, and Adamache 1988).

In their evaluation of the Medicare competition demonstrations, involving the performance of 26 HMOs and CMPs between 1982 and 1984, Langwell and Hadley (1989) did not find that HMOs and CMPs had saved costs. The authors caution, though, that the demonstration HMOs and CMPs may not have been representative of risk-contracting HMOs in the Medicare program.

Medicare provides health care coverage for those over the age of 65 who would generally have a difficult time securing coverage in the private sector. Medicare, however, has a number of characteristics that detract from the efficiency and equity of the program. First, higher-income individuals pay a lesser proportion of their income than lower-income individuals to finance the program. Second, high-income individuals receive the same benefits as low-income individuals. Third, generally all hospitals are paid the same rate per DRG and cannot achieve a larger market share by offering lower prices to the government. Moreover, DRGs only apply to inpatient hospital services and exclude outpatient services, physician services, tests, and outpatient pharmaceuticals.

Expenditures for Medicare have grown enormously since its inception in 1966. One may question the cost effectiveness of spending an increasingly larger share of the health care budget on people who are over 65 when a significant proportion of people under age 65 do not have health insurance at all. Moreover, to compound this anomaly, a large proportion of the Medicare budget (more than 28 percent) is accounted for by individuals in their last year of life (Lubitz and Prihoda 1984).

Medicaid

Medicaid, established with Medicare in 1965, provides health care coverage to a number of economically disadvantaged groups. It is not a national program but a joint effort between the individual states (except for Arizona, which has its own program to provide health services for the indigent) and the federal government, with the federal government paying more than half of the medical services and administrative costs. States' contributions to the program vary according to their per capita income, and each state establishes its own criteria for Medicaid eligibility and benefit levels. In effect, a distinct Medicaid program exists for each state, the District of Columbia, and each of the five territories.

In total, all of the Medicaid programs provided coverage to approximately 40 percent of individuals falling below the national poverty level in 1986 (Congressional Research Service 1988, 5). Moreover, because Medicaid is primarily based on eligibility categories rather than on income or need, one-quarter of the people who received Medicaid were in families that exceeded the national poverty level (Congressional Research Service 1988, 269).

Nearly four-fifths of Medicaid beneficiaries qualify for assistance by virtue of receiving assistance through two other programs: Aid to

Families with Dependent Children (AFDC), which supplements the income of needy children and their relatives, and the provisions of the Supplemental Security Income (SSI) program, which provides cash payments for the aged, blind, and disabled. Individuals who are "medically needy" because they have used their assets and income for medical expenses are also eligible for Medicaid assistance if they fit into the AFDC and SSI categories. Individuals can only qualify for coverage under each of these categories if they have inadequate income as judged by the state in which they reside. At their own option, without federal matching assistance, states may also cover individuals who, for example, are eligible for "general assistance under a statewide program." By and large, however, single persons, childless persons, and families with two able-bodied parents are not covered by Medicaid regardless of income level, unless a state specifically decides to enroll them.

Since each state has the responsibility for setting coverage levels, it is not surprising to observe substantial state-to-state variation in covered services. In general, state Medicaid programs must pay for physician services, inpatient and outpatient hospital care, diagnostic services, laboratory and x-ray services, family planning services, and skilled nursing facilities. The largest component of Medicaid spending has been for long-term care services, which account for nearly 38 percent of Medicaid expenditures. The terms under which states receive federal funds for Medicaid programs forbid requiring copayments or deductibles of beneficiaries.

Medicaid expenditures differ among states because of variability in coverage levels, eligibility requirements, and reimbursement patterns. New York had Medicaid expenses of $381.67 per capita in 1984, while Wyoming paid $52.05 per capita. The average state payment per capita was $147.81 (Holahan and Cohen 1986, 18, 19). The Medicaid expenditure per recipient was $3,069.60 in New York in 1984, but only $737.62 in West Virginia. The U.S. average expenditure per recipient was $1,716.99 (Holahan and Cohen 1986, 18, 19). The range in Medicaid expenditures is not unexpected given the variation in eligibility requirements among the states. For example, in 1988 the maximum per capita income for a family of three for Medicaid eligibility ranged from 14.61 percent of the U.S. poverty level in Alabama to 74.67 percent in Vermont and 77.19 percent in Alaska (Congressional Research Service 1988, 269). In general, the states with the highest income had the largest expenditures (Holahan and Cohen 1986, 25).

Medicaid expenditures and reimbursement strategies

Medicaid expenditures have increased substantially between 1970 and 1986. The number of Medicaid beneficiaries has also increased, but expenditures per beneficiary have increased at a greater rate. Since 1981, however, total expenditures for Medicaid and expenditures per Medicaid beneficiary have increased at a much slower rate. Table 6.3 shows the expenditures for Medicaid, the number of Medicaid beneficiaries, and expenditures per beneficiary for selected years from 1970 through 1986. During those years, expenditures per beneficiary increased nearly 400 percent.

Table 6.3 Medicaid Expenditures and Beneficiaries, 1970–1986

Fiscal Year	*Expenditures (in millions)*	*Beneficiaries (in thousands)*	*Expenditures per Beneficiary*
1970	$ 5,094	14,507	$ 351
1975	12,242	22,007	556
1980	23,311	21,605	1,079
1985	37,508	21,814	1,719
1986	41,027	22,518	1,822

Source: Congressional Research Service (1988). *Medicaid Source Book: Background Data and Analysis*, Washington, DC: U.S. Government Printing Office, Table 1–1, p. 20.

State governments have used a number of innovative approaches to contain the costs of their Medicaid programs. For example, the Omnibus Budget Reconciliation Act of 1981 (PL 97–35) allowed states, for the first time, to limit the beneficiary's choice of providers. In addition, many states require prior authorization for certain procedures and nonemergency admissions (Zuckerman 1987). Most states have switched to prospective reimbursement; by August 1987, only seven states and the District of Columbia used a cost-based payment system (Congressional Research Service 1988, 125). In 1987, 14 states used the DRG system (Congressional Research Service 1988, 125, 126).

A large number of physicians will not accept Medicaid patients because Medicaid generally reimburses below competitive levels (Grannemann and Pauly 1983). Access to health care services, however, is not entirely impeded since individuals who have Medicaid coverage may continue to receive care at outpatient sites such as clinics, hospital outpatient departments, or hospital emergency rooms (Long, Settle, and

Stuart 1986). Fees are usually limited to the lesser of the actual charges of physicians or an amount determined by a state fee schedule. Further, states have reduced the fees they pay in an attempt to contain their Medicaid outlays, and neither physicians nor the states can recoup any funds through patient payments as copayments and deductibles are forbidden. In those states in which Medicaid pays physicians on a fee-for-service basis, however, there is no cap on total physician payments.

In order to test alternative financing mechanisms for improving access of Medicaid enrollees to the health care system, six states—California, Florida, Minnesota, Missouri, New Jersey, and New York—began to limit choice of physician in 1982. In addition, each of the programs contained a case-management provision in which the state contracted with primary care organizations or with a prepaid health plan on a capitated basis. Preliminary evidence indicates that the case-management approach may provide care in a more organized fashion than the traditional fee-for-service approach, while reducing unnecessary services. Cost savings, however, were small (Freund et al. 1989).

The California and Arizona programs

In contrast to the regulatory approach used by most of the states, California and Arizona have instituted a competitive approach to containing health care costs that is much more encompassing than the six-state demonstration project described above. In California, selective contracting attempts to contain hospital and physician expenditures in a very different framework than the DRG payment system or any other prospective payment system. Under a prospective payment system, the government as buyer sets a single price for each of a variety of inpatient services for all hospitals. Under the California selective contracting system, each hospital submits to the state government a bid in terms of a per diem rate for inpatient services for Medicaid (termed "Medi-Cal" in California) patients.

The state selects Medi-Cal provider hospitals based on the per diem rate bidders submit and the degree of quality and access they provide. Teaching hospitals (perhaps as proxies for hospitals with high-quality care) and hospitals that already have a high Medi-Cal census (perhaps as proxies for hospitals offering good access to care) are especially likely to receive Medi-Cal contracts (Brown, Cousineau, and Price 1985). Unlike hospitals reimbursed under the DRG system, hospitals that bid successfully to become Medi-Cal providers will increase their number of Medicaid patients (Johns, Anderson, and Derzon 1985).

California adopted selective contracting for inpatient hospital care in July 1982 and for physician services and outpatient care in July 1983. In the first year, more than two-thirds of all hospitals received Medi-Cal contracts (Johns, Anderson, and Derzon 1985). Johns, Anderson, and Derzon (1985) have found that cost increases by hospitals have been moderate with no decline in access or quality of care. Holahan and Cohen (1986) have suggested, however, that the moderation of costs may have been due to the implementation of Medi-Cal's preadmission review and concurrent review programs rather than due to selective contracting. Physician fees appear to be reduced under a combination of selective contracting and the large number of private-sector preferred provider organizations in California. In addition, beneficiaries' access to physicians appears to have been preserved, even though some hospitals have had to close because of the pressures of selective contracting (Johns and Jones 1987, 68; Johns, Anderson, and Derzon 1985, 345).

In Arizona since 1982, under the Arizona Health Care Cost Containment System (AHCCCS), bids have been solicited from health care organizations for prepaid comprehensive capitation contracts for acute care services for needy individuals (Christianson, Hillman, and Smith 1983). Bids have been submitted both by private firms and by some Arizona counties that provided medical care for the indigent prior to the establishment of AHCCCS. Among the winning bidders in the fourth year of operation were for-profit and nonprofit individual practice associations, group- and staff-model health maintenance organizations, and county-sponsored plans (McCall et al. 1987).

Prior to AHCCCS, there was no statewide Medicaid program. AHCCCS is still considered a Health Care Financing Administration demonstration project, and long-term care services, for example, which must be covered by states that participate in Medicaid, are not covered in Arizona. Moreover, unlike other Medicaid programs, AHCCCS expects beneficiaries to make copayments for acute care health services (McCall et al. 1987).

A number of considerations are important in Arizona's selection of capitated plans. The financial viability, access to providers, and year-to-year continuity of care that plans offer appear to be more important than the actual dollar amounts of their bids. The state also appears to be reluctant to change plans under contract unless a new plan has a decidedly lower bid. (Individuals, however, may switch plans after a year.) To monitor quality of care, each winning plan must have a quality assurance program that is audited by the state (McCall et al. 1987; Schaller, Bostrom, and Rafferty 1986).

Medicaid risk-based systems and case management alternatives

By 1987, approximately 1 million Medicaid beneficiaries were enrolled in a capitated system (Congressional Research Service 1988, 150). Medicaid beneficiaries usually have the option of either enrolling in a capitated system or receiving care on a traditional fee-for-service basis, although enrollment in a capitation program is mandatory in some states (Hurley and Freund 1988). Both federally qualified HMOs and HMOs that are not federally qualified but certified by the state may enroll Medicaid beneficiaries. Prepaid health plans that are community or regional health centers and meet federal requirements may also enroll Medicaid beneficiaries. States still have the task of determining the per capita payment rate, as Medicare must do for its enrollees. Often, a capitated plan will designate a primary physician as gatekeeper or case manager in order to control access to specialty and tertiary components of the plan. The gatekeeper may be at financial risk under the capitation contract or may practice fee-for-service medicine.

Gatekeepers have the responsibility of referring patients to physicians throughout the health care system. Gatekeepers may also refer patients to hospitals and coordinate home care, long-term care, and rehabilitative services. Gatekeepers may assume full, partial, or no risk for health care expenditures that exceed the per capita payment rate (Kern 1986).

The gatekeeper may provide some benefits for the patient in locating specialist physicians as well as in avoiding duplication of care. Hurley and Freund (1988) suggest that the largest potential savings of the gatekeeper may be the reduction in expensive emergency room use.

Medicaid and long-term care expenditures

The largest share of Medicaid expenditures, approximately 43 percent, is for nursing home care. Nursing homes, however, need not be synonymous with institutions that benefit the elderly, nor is nursing home care synonymous with all of long-term care. For example, 12 percent of Medicaid expenditures goes for intermediate care facilities for the mentally retarded (Gornick, Greenberg, Eggers, and Dobson 1985). In addition, increasingly since the enactment of the Omnibus Budget Reconciliation Act of 1981, Medicaid has paid for home health care and community-based health care, as well as adult day care for the elderly. More than 90 percent of Medicaid long-term care expenditures, however, is for nursing home care (Meltzer 1988).

As is true for acute care expenditures, Medicaid expenditures for long-term care vary enormously among the states. In 1986, for instance, Medicaid spent $1,942 per beneficiary in Alabama and $11,303 per beneficiary in New York (Congressional Research Service 1988).

Medicaid is the dominant payer in the nursing home industry, accounting for 42 percent of nursing home expenditures in 1985 (Swan, Harrington, and Grant 1988). Medicare, on the other hand, paid less than 5 percent of nursing home costs, usually after an acute care episode. Private insurance also paid for less than 5 percent of nursing home costs. The remainder of nursing home costs were paid by individuals without public or private insurance.

Eligibility standards for long-term care

Each state, within federal guidelines, sets its own eligibility standards for long-term care as it does for acute care. Individuals are generally eligible for Medicaid long-term care benefits if they are categorically needy under the SSI program. Individuals may become eligible for Medicaid after enrolling in a nursing home and subsequently spending nearly all of their assets and wealth on the home (the spend-down effect). If a spouse is alive, he or she may also become impoverished although he or she may not reside in a nursing home.

States have attempted to contain long-term care expenditures in a number of different ways. They have paid nursing homes on a prospective, cost-based system rather than on a retrospective basis; paid nursing homes a flat per diem rate; paid for lower-cost substitutes such as home care; created continuing care retirement communities; and grouped all long-term care facilities and institutions into a large social/health maintenance organization (S/HMO) similar to an acute care health maintenance organization. States have grouped individuals into resource utilization groups in order to consider the differences in resources needed to care for the elderly. Certificate-of-need laws have been enacted in a number of states to limit the supply of nursing home beds. Finally, states have simply paid less for nursing home care than what might be charged for private-pay individuals.

The results of these programs have been mixed. It appears that flat-rate reimbursement has had a positive effect on reducing the rate of increase in nursing home costs (Intergovernmental Health Policy Project 1987; Holahan 1985). Certificate-of-need programs have limited the number of new nursing homes and nursing home beds; on the other hand, the programs have also given existing nursing homes some monopoly power by limiting the supply of facilities. Further, reimbursement of nursing homes at below the competitive rate of payment has made it less likely that they will accept Medicaid beneficiaries.

Summary of the Medicaid program

A primary goal of the Medicaid program was to enhance access to health care by the poor. The program has succeeded, in part, by increasing physician utilization by some of the indigent. Davis (1976) reported that, two years prior to the beginning of the Medicaid program "high-income individuals saw physicians about 20 percent more frequently than the poor." By 1974, however, "low-income individuals saw physicians . . . more frequently than high-income people" (Davis 1976). Davis (1976) also reported that poor children increased the frequency of their physician visits between 1964 and 1974. Nevertheless, by the mid-1980s, approximately 40 percent of individuals below the nation's poverty level were not eligible for Medicaid. In contrast, 25 percent of those who received Medicaid were above the national poverty level.

If a goal of Medicaid is to increase access to health care by the poor, a more efficient way to achieve that goal may be to provide Medicaid benefits to those who are below the poverty level in terms of assets or wealth. In addition, there are individuals who may not have income or assets below the poverty level but may have high medical expenses relative to income. Moreover, the low payments for physician services has had an adverse effect on access for those who are elegible for Medicaid coverage.

There appears to be a great deal of diversity in cost-containment efforts among the 50 states. Only a few states are still using retrospective reimbursement. The majority of the states are using prospective reimbursement, and California and Arizona (as discussed above) are using competitive, selective bidding. Managed care appears to be an integral part of many cost-containment efforts. The state of Oregon has even begun to ration care in its Medicaid program (see Chapter 10). It is unclear why different states have elected to use different doses of competition and regulation (and this would make a fruitful topic for future research), although studies have suggested that increases in costs have engendered increases in cost-containment measures (Fanara and Greenberg 1985).

The bulk of Medicaid expenditures is for long-term care. By paying a rate below the competitive level to nursing homes, Medicaid has limited its beneficiaries' access to and choice of nursing homes. A beneficiary must pass a means test to be eligible for Medicaid, which means that nursing home residents are subject to strict spend-down requirements. In addition, most Medicaid programs have been reluctant, perhaps because of moral hazard, to expend funds for community-based care, a reluctance that presses further on the demand for more costly nursing homes. Add to these factors the reality of an increasingly aged population, and it is not surprising that long-term care costs continue to increase.

References

Anderson, G. F., Steinberg, E. P., Holloway, J., and Cantor, J. C. (1986). "Paying for HMO Care: Issues and Options in Setting Capitation Rates," *The Milbank Quarterly* 64 (no. 4): 548–65.

Brown, E. R., Cousineau, M. R., and Price, W. P. (1985). "Competing for Medi-Cal Business: Why Hospitals Did, and Did Not, Get Contracts," *Inquiry* 22: 237–50.

Christianson, J. B., Hillman, D. G., and Smith, K. R. (1983). "The Arizona Experiment: Competitive Bidding for Indigent Medical Care," *Health Affairs* 2: 88–104.

Congressional Research Service for Use of Subcommittee on Health of the Committee on Energy and Commerce (1988). *Medicaid Source Book: Background Data and Analysis.* Washington, DC: U.S. Government Printing Office.

Davis, K. (1976). "Medicaid Payments and Utilization of Medical Services by the Poor," *Inquiry* 13: 122–35.

Fanara, P., Jr., and Greenberg, W. (1985). "Factors Affecting the Adoption of Prospective Reimbursement Programs by State Governments." In *Incentives vs. Controls in Health Policy*, ed. J. Meyer, 144–56. Washington, DC: American Enterprise Institute.

Freund, D. A. et al. (1989). "Evaluations of the Medicaid Competition Demonstrations," *Health Care Financing Review* 11 (no. 2): 81–97.

Gabel, J. R., and Rice, T. H. (1985). "Reducing Public Expenditures for Physician Services: The Price of Paying Less," *Journal of Health Politics, Policy and Law* 9: 605–09.

Gornick, M., Greenberg, J. N., Eggers, P. W., and Dobson, A. (1985). "Twenty Years of Medicare and Medicaid: Covered Populations, Use of Benefits, and Program Expenditures," *Health Care Financing Review* Annual Supplement: 13–59.

Grannemann, T. W., and Pauly, M. V. (1983). *Controlling Medicaid Costs.* Washington, DC: American Enterprise Institute.

Health Care Financing Administration (1987). *The Medicare and Medicaid Data Book, 1986.* Baltimore, MD: U.S. Government Printing Office.

Holahan, J. F. (1985). "State Rate-Setting and Its Effects on the Cost of Nursing Home Care," *Journal of Health Politics, Policy and Law* 9: 647–67.

Holahan, J. F., and Cohen, J. W. (1986). *Medicaid: The Trade-off Between Cost Containment and Access to Care.* Washington, DC: Urban Institute.

Horn, S. et al. (1985). "Interhospital Differences in Severity of Illness," *New England Journal of Medicine* 313: 20–24.

Hsiao, W. C., Braun, P., Yntema, D., and Becker, E. (1988). "Estimating Physicians' Work for a Resource-Based Relative Value Scale," *New England Journal of Medicine* 319: 835–41.

Hurley, R. E., and Freund, D. A. (1988). "A Typology of Medicaid Managed Care," *Medical Care* 26: 764–73.

Intergovernmental Health Policy Project (1987). *Comparative Survey of Medicaid Reimbursement Systems for Long-Term Care Services, State-by-State,* 1980–1985. Washington, DC.

Johns, L., Anderson, M., and Derzon, R. A. (1985). "Selective Contracting in California: Experience in the Second Year," *Inquiry* 22: 335–47.

Johns, L., and Jones, M. W. (1987). "Physician Response to Selective Contracting in California," *Health Affairs* 6: 59–69.

Kern, R. G. (1986). "The Unfinished Agenda for Medicaid Reform." In *Medicaid and Other Experiments in State Health Policy,* eds. R. G. Kern and S. R. Windham, 51–52. Washington, DC: American Enterprise Institute.

Langwell, K. M., and Hadley, J. M. (1989). "Evaluation of the Medicare Competition Demonstrations," *Health Care Financing Review* 11 (no. 2): 65–80.

Long, S. H., Settle, R., and Stuart, B. (1986). "Reimbursement and Access to Physicians' Services under Medicaid," *Journal of Health Economics* 5: 235–51.

Lubitz, J., and Prihoda, R. (1984). "The Use and Costs of Medicare Services in the Last 2 Years of Life," *Health Care Financing Review* 5: 117–31.

McCall, N., et al. (1987). "Evaluation of Arizona Health Care Cost Containment System, 1984–85," *Health Care Financing Review* 7: 77–88.

Meltzer, J. W. (1988). "Financing Long-Term Care: A Major Obstacle to Reform." In *The Economics and Ethics of Long-Term Care and Disability,* eds. S. Sullivan and M. E. Lewin, 56–72. Washington, DC: American Enterprise Institute.

Merlis, M. (1988). *Medicare: Risk Contracts with Health Maintenance Organizations and Competitive Medical Plans.* Washington, DC: Congressional Research Service.

Modern Healthcare (1989). "Record 81 Hospitals Close," *Modern Healthcare* 19 (no. 3): 2.

Newhouse, J. P., and Byne, D. J. (1988). "Did Medicare's Prospective Payment System Cause Length-of-Stay to Fall?" *Journal of Health Economics* 7: 413–16.

Noll, R., and Enthoven, A. C. (1984). "Prospective Payment: Will it Solve Medicare's Financial Problem?" *Issues in Science and Technology* 1: 101–16.

Physician Payment Review Commission (1988). *Annual Report to Congress.* Washington, DC: U.S. Government Printing Office.

Prospective Payment Assessment Commission (1991). *Report and Recommendations to the Congress.* Washington, DC.

———. (1990a). *Medicare Prospective Payment and the American Health Care System.* Washington, DC.

———.(1990b). *Report and Recommendations to the Secretary, U.S. Department of Health and Human Services.* Washington, DC.

Rossiter, L., and Langwell, K. (1988). "Medicare's Two Systems for Paying Providers," *Health Affairs* 7: 120–32.

Rossiter, L. F., Nelson, L. M., and Adamache, K. W. (1988). "Service Use and Costs for Medicare Beneficiaries in Risk-based HMO's and CMP's: Some Interim Results from the National Medicare Competition Evaluation," *American Journal of Public Health* 78: 937–43.

Schaller, D. F., Bostrom, A. W., and Rafferty, J. (1986). "Quality of Care Review: Recent Experience in Arizona," *Health Care Financing Review* Annual Supplement: 65–74.

Sloan, F. A., Morrisey, M. A., and Valvona, J. (1988). "Effects of the Medicare Prospective Payment System on Hospital Cost Containment: An Early Appraisal," *Milbank Quarterly* 66 (no. 2): 191–220.

Sobaski, W. (1989). Personal correspondence.

Swan, J. H., Harrington, C., and Grant, L. A. (1988). "State Medicaid Reimbursement for Nursing Homes, 1978–1986," *Health Care Financing Review* 9 (no. 3): 33–50.

U.S. Congress, Committee on Ways and Means (1990). *Overview of Entitlement Programs; Background Material and Data on Programs within the Jurisdiction of the Committee on Ways and Means,* 101st Congress, 2nd session.

U.S. Congress, Congressional Budget Office (1988). *Including Capital Expenses in the Prospective Payment System.* Washington, DC: Congressional Budget Office.

Zuckerman, S. (1987). "Medicaid Hospital Spending: Effects of Reimbursement and Utilization Control Policies," *Health Care Financing Review* 9: 65–77.

7

Regulation versus Competition in Health Care

In nearly all industries there has been or continues to be some form of regulatory activity by the government. Regulation of rates, quotas, tariffs, and licensing has been common in American history. Taxicab rates, airline safety, utility prices, and the size of farm output have been regulated. Government regulation also pervades the health care sector.

This chapter first examines the form that regulation takes in the economy in general and why regulation exists in American industries. To what extent, for example, are there political as well as economic reasons for regulation? Second, this chapter examines various forms of health care regulation, including regulation of entry, price, health insurance, and information. Finally, this chapter will examine the role of competition in the health care sector. It will examine competition first among providers and then among various forms of health insurance plans and alternative delivery systems. The chapter concludes with a discussion on the potential limits of competition in achieving a more efficient and equitable health care system.

Government Regulation of Industries Other than Health Care

Government regulation takes several forms. One form is price regulation of a firm's output. In 1887, for example, the Interstate Commerce Commission began establishing the minimum railroad charges for interstate freight shipments. Later, price regulation was extended to common carrier trucking, water carriers, and pipelines, before the gradual deregulation of the 1980s (Glaskowsky 1986). In addition, government purchases of "surplus" agricultural production have created artificially high prices for such farm products as wheat, corn, and tobacco.

Regulation of prices has occurred outside the transportation and agricultural sectors as well. Even the price of money (the interest rate) for time and savings accounts has been regulated by the board of governors of the Federal Reserve System and the Federal Deposit Insurance Corporation so that rates would not exceed a certain level. In 1980 the Depository Institutions Deregulation and Monetary Control Act eliminated the artificially imposed interest rate ceilings on deposit accounts for depository institutions (Cooper and Fraser 1984).

Another form of government regulation limits new competition or creates barriers to entry into industries. The regulation of imports (import quotas) or the imposition of tariffs (taxes on foreign commodities) hampers competition from foreign firms. The Civil Aeronautics Board, in addition to discouraging price competition, regulated entry of new airline carriers to the extent that not a single new trunk line entered the market for airline services from the creation of the board in 1938 until its gradual abolishment beginning in 1978 (Morrison and Winston 1986).

Economists have suggested that the prices set by the regulatory authorities are not socially optimal since it is unlikely that the government would be able to compute the marginal costs and marginal revenue of each individual firm in order to set economically efficient prices. Moreover, entry restrictions enable firms to set prices at an artificially high level, which results in higher profits than if the industry were more competitive. Regulation of the output of the existing firms in an industry attempts to ensure that prices and profits will be higher than the competitive level. Output regulation limits the quantity of goods and services that firms can produce. In agriculture, the government regulates the amount of acreage that can be set aside for the production of various crops.

In addition to regulations that affect price directly, there are regulations that affect price indirectly. Firms that pollute the environment, for example, engender externalities or costs that the public as a whole must bear. To account for the social costs of pollution, government may mandate that firms install pollution devices, or it may impose taxes on firms that pollute. If firms have relatively inelastic demand curves, they may be able to pass the increased costs of pollution devices and taxes on to customers in the form of higher prices.

Safety regulations imposed on firms also affect price. For example, the Federal Aviation Administration requires certain standards of safety on airplanes. By requiring seat belts, qualification standards for pilots, and construction standards and maintenance on airplanes, these regulations affect costs directly and prices indirectly.

Another form of regulation that affects price indirectly is rate-of-return regulation of utilities such as natural gas, water, and electric power. A utility usually experiences a decline in its long-run average costs as it produces more units. This is due to the high fixed costs of the capital investment of the firm. Such economies of scale may allow only one firm to survive in the industry as a natural monopoly since it could reduce prices below those of its competitors. As a monopoly, the firm would be able to charge a monopoly price. To prevent the firm from realizing an excessive rate of return from a monopoly price, rates of return are regulated.

Some economists suggest that regulation may also stem from the demand for regulation in the political marketplace, aside from any imperfections in the economic marketplace. That is, industries may be regulated because firms in the industry desire to have the protection of government regulation to curb competitive pressures from inside or outside the industry (Peltzman 1976; Stigler 1971). It usually is in the interest of existing firms to have their prices regulated, to restrict entry, or to limit production in order to gain higher profits. Furthermore, existing firms may have considerable political influence over government legislation and the regulatory process (Peltzman 1976; Stigler 1971). The farm industry has been most outspoken in demanding governmental restrictions on agricultural outputs, automobile manufacturers have demanded restrictions on the import of foreign automobiles, and the trucking industry has supported rate regulation.

Regulation in the Health Care Sector

What have been the types of regulation in health care and what have been the effects of the regulation? As in industries in other sectors, regulations in health care industries may restrict entry and limit prices. In addition, health insurance firms have received special regulatory attention. Regulations have also been enacted to restrict the supply of information to consumers and to attempt to improve safety in health care products and services.

Regulations that restrict entry into provider markets

There are a number of regulations that restrict entry into the hospital, physician, alternative delivery system, and nursing home markets. In 1910, the so-called Flexner Report, written by educator Abraham

Flexner and the Carnegie Foundation for the Advancement of Teaching, recommended a reduction in the number of medical schools and medical students in order to improve the quality of medical care. The American Medical Association used this report as justification to limit the number of medical school graduates (Kessel 1958). Since the AMA had already received from the states the responsibility to certify or accredit medical schools, it was able to decertify medical schools, while ostensibly increasing the quality of care. Between 1906 and 1944, it closed 93 medical schools (Kessel 1958). As described in Chapter 2, the AMA placed further restrictions on paramedicals and alternative delivery systems.

State certificate-of-need laws enacted in the mid–1970s regulated the number of hospital beds, the dollar value of hospital equipment, and the number of nursing homes. Proponents of certificate-of-need laws believed that an increase in the number of hospital beds would increase costs, since empty beds would be more likely to be filled. Moreover, hospitals appeared to compete by purchasing new technologies to attract physicians who, in turn, would admit patients. If there were a limit to the acquisition of new technology, the total costs of new technology by all hospitals would be smaller.

Certificate-of-need laws, however, may serve to protect the interests of existing hospitals by limiting the expansion of competitors or entry of new hospitals. Many states, in legislation opposed by many hospitals, have now abandoned certificate-of-need laws because studies revealed that certificate of need did little to reduce total hospital investment. In states where certificate-of-need laws appeared to limit the growth of new beds, hospitals increased their investment in new facilities and equipment (Salkever and Bice 1976). Joskow (1981) also found that certificate-of-need regulation had no effect on either the level or the rate of growth of hospital expenditures.

Historically, state legislation in the form of "freedom-of-choice" laws specified that groups of physicians or groups of hospitals could not be formed by employers, insuring organizations, or any other groups, to compete against the remaining physicians or hospitals in the state. Until freedom-of-choice laws were repealed, preferred provider organizations and some staff-model health maintenance organizations could not be established (Weller 1984). Prior to the passage of the Omnibus Budget Reconciliation Act of 1981 (PL 97–35), the Medicaid program allowed its beneficiaries to choose whichever provider they preferred. After 1981, most states gave their Medicaid beneficiaries the option of selecting preferred provider organizations. Beneficiaries who joined PPOs would be limited to selecting the providers offered by the organization.

As we shall see in Chapter 9, certificate-of-need laws have been used in the nursing home industry to restrict the entry of new homes, much to the benefit of existing homes. The result has been lower quality and higher prices than would have been the case without restrictions.

Regulation of price

Price regulation has been extensive in health care, perhaps more so than in any other sector. There may be a number of reasons for this. First, rapidly increasing costs in health care may have affected the amount of regulation. State governments paying an increasing amount for health services (primarily Medicaid) had, of course, less money available for other state programs and, therefore, faced increasing pressures to reduce health care expenditures (Fanara and Greenberg 1985).

Furthermore, price regulation may have sprung from the greater political power of the nonprofit hospitals relative to for-profit hospitals. One study has shown that prospective reimbursement or price regulation is inversely related to the percentage of for-profit hospital beds in a state (Fanara and Greenberg 1985). Nonprofit hospitals may have desired to have the prices of all hospitals regulated rather than contend with any potential offers by for-profits to cut prices to the third-party insuring organizations or alternative delivery systems.

Most of the regulation of price has been in the hospital and nursing home industries, although there was regulation of physician prices or fees in the early 1970s under the Economic Stabilization Program. Regulation of physician prices or fees at that time may have been prompted by the large rate of increase in such fees.

What have been the form and the effects of price regulation in health care? In Chapter 6, we discussed the effects of DRG regulation, a form of price regulation, on costs. The evidence suggests that the cost per admission to hospitals was about the same before and after the implementation of the DRG system, although there was a significant reduction in the number of hospital admissions after DRG implementation. Outpatient costs, however, escalated at a much-greater rate.

In addition, the states have instituted a number of prospective price controls on hospitals, although, in effect, these have been mostly revenue or cost controls since it appears that the largest increases in hospital costs have stemmed mostly from increases in utilization rather than increases in prices. In 1977, nine states utilized mandatory prospective reimbursement systems (Fanara and Greenberg 1985). Other states regulated only hospital charges. Sloan (1983) examined the effects these state regulatory programs had on costs. In general, he found very little effect in initial years but a substantial effect in reducing cost per admission thereafter. Sloan attributed the delay to the increase in regulatory expertise that the government gained after the first years of cost containment. However, one might also expect that the regulated hospitals would, after a learning period, gain insights into the most effective ways to avoid cost containment and therefore escape from under the regulatory umbrella.

Joskow (1981 255), in his examination of the mandatory state prospective reimbursement programs, found "a significant reduction in the rate of growth of hospital expenditures." He cautioned, however, that many of the states that had introduced cost containment were high-cost states and perhaps the states in which costs could be curbed most readily.

Very few studies have examined the effects of price regulation on the quality of care, innovation, and market power of hospitals. Shortell and Hughes (1988) have found a significant, positive relationship between the stringency of state hospital rate-review programs (as well as the intensity of competition) and inpatient mortality rates for 16 selected clinical conditions. Fewer resources may have been utilized for hospital patients, although as the authors point out, mortality rates are not a complete measure of quality of care.

Insurance regulation

The insurance industry is primarily regulated on a state-by-state basis. Since individuals purchase most insurance with the expectation that they will have coverage for at least a year, state governments have attempted to assure the solvency of insurance firms. Many states, therefore, regulate the level of insurance premiums to assure adequate assets and reserves. These regulations may reduce or eliminate bankruptcies, but they may also guarantee the survival of the least efficient insurance firms.

In many states, insurance firms are also required to offer certain benefits as part of the benefit package. Mandated benefits are usually outside the scope of hospital and physician benefits and might include, for example, a specified number of visits to psychologists or chiropractors. The effect of mandated benefits is to shift the demand curve for health services upward and to the right, which would, at least initially, prompt an increase in price for these services. The effects of mandated benefits on employers might be equivalent to the effects of increases in the minimum wage (Summers 1989; Brown 1988). Increases in minimum wages, according to Brown (1988), may increase unemployment because of their positive effect on labor costs.

Blue Cross and Blue Shield plans have been regulated to a much greater extent than the commercial insurers. Not only do most states regulate Blues premiums, but many states require the Blues to have open-enrollment periods for anyone willing to pay a regulated nongroup rate. Preexisting conditions are generally not covered by Blues plans for at least one year. There are no currently available data on the number of Blue Cross and Blue Shield plans with regulated premiums or open-enrollment periods.

The effects of regulating Blue Cross and Blue Shield are mixed. There is evidence that at least some Blues plans enroll a greater number of high-risk individuals (and a greater proportion) than the commercial insurers (Greenberg 1989). Fanara and Greenberg (1985) found, however, that the more competition that Blue Cross and Blue Shield face from HMOs, the less likely they are to enroll high-risk individuals. It is not clear that an increase in the enrollment of high-risk individuals is sufficient to justify the exemption from health insurance premium, property, and income taxes that Blue Cross and Blue Shield enjoy.

Finally, all insurers are exempt from antitrust prosecution under the McCarran-Ferguson Act (15 USC 1011-1015) of 1945 to the extent that the "business of insurance" is regulated by the states. For example, under the aegis of state regulation, insurance firms may share loss information, which may be critical to setting premium rates. Agreements by some firms to boycott, coerce, or intimidate other firms in the industry are not immune from the Sherman Act, however. Since it appears that some firms could not compete in this industry without the antitrust exemption, this exemption may keep inefficient firms in the market with premiums higher than would be the case in a competitive market.

If smaller, more inefficient firms did not have the antitrust exemption and either went out of business or grew to a larger size, economies of scale might be realized in both health administration and cost containment. Blair, Jackson, and Vogel (1975) have reported economies of scale in the administration of health insurance, and Feldman and Greenberg (1981) have also found economies of scale in cost containment.

Regulation to restrict the flow of information to consumers

In the eyeglass industry, advertising has been prohibited by many states. Benham (1972) showed that prices of eyeglasses were higher in the states that prohibited advertising since firms could not realize economies of scale by lowering prices and gaining greater market share. In an update of the Benham study, Kwoka (1984) found that not only were prices lower with advertising but also average market quality was better. This is because both advertisers and nonadvertisers dropped their prices, and to compete more effectively with the lower-priced advertisers, nonadvertisers raised their quality.

The purpose of health care regulation

Unlike the regulation of natural gas, electric, and water utilities, regulation in health care does not exist because of economies of scale. Although a single hospital may experience some economies of scale in a particular local area, generally there is enough competition from hospitals in other local areas as well as from ambulatory care units to prevent a single hospital from becoming a monopoly.

While in some sectors of the economy externalities like pollution give rise to government regulations, no government regulations of providers in health care are due to externalities or social costs. In contrast, there are government subsidies to scientific research, which may provide long-term health care benefits to society as a whole (social benefits). Government may also immunize children, at low cost, against contagious diseases that could affect society as a whole.

Safety regulation is common in health care as in many complex industries. For example, the Food and Drug Administration regulates pharmaceutical firms such that new drugs must undergo extensive tests until they are shown to be safe and effective for public use. In addition, there are state regulations of hospitals and nursing homes to ensure that cleanliness and size of room are adequate. Finally, as noted, in health care industries as in other industries there are regulations to exempt firms or groups of firms from competition.

Competition in the Health Care Sector

What forms has competition taken in health care? Because of the presence of insurance, health care competition exists on two levels: competition among providers and competition among insuring organizations.

Competition among providers

Although insurance pays for two-thirds of health care expenditures, there is still competition among providers. Chapter 8 describes antitrust cases involving physicians who would not allow competing physicians staff privileges at hospitals. In addition, more than 200,000 physicians are associated with preferred provider organizations, which compete with fee-for-service physicians (American Medical Care and Review Association 1988, Table ii, p. xxvi). There is evidence (see Chapter 2) of physicians who have relocated from areas with high physician-to-population ratios into less competitive rural areas (Williams, Schwartz, Newhouse, and Bennet 1983). Pauly (1978) also suggests that there is price-based competition among physicians such as pediatricians, whose services generally are not well covered by insurance.

Competition exists between hospitals and surgicenters and among hospitals. Chapter 8 describes the difficulties that some surgicenters may experience in delivering their services in areas that are near hospitals. More than 2,700 of the nation's 5,700 nonfederal, short-term, acute care hospitals are associated with preferred provider organizations (American Medical Care and Review Association 1988). There is also a large amount of nonprice competition among hospitals. Hospitals, of course, have always competed by purchasing the most advanced forms of technological equipment. Recent evidence suggests that hospital markets encompass a larger geographic area and face a greater number of competitors than formerly recognized (Morrisey, Sloan, and Valvona 1988). Except for preferred provider organizations, however, there has been no evidence of price competition among hospitals.

Competition among insuring organizations

Many economists believe that competition among insuring organizations may be the best avenue for improving the allocation of health care resources. Two of the most important factors in a competitive framework—factors not generally present when patients choose among providers—are present in competition among health-insuring organizations. First, buyers of health plans (whether employers or individuals) may be sensitive to prices of health-insuring organizations since purchases are not influenced by the distortions of insurance. (To the extent that the employer only offers one health plan or pays the full cost of each plan that is offered, individuals, of course, will not be sensitive.) Second, buyers of health plans generally can make an informed choice in deciding which plan to purchase.

Health plans may be traditional, indemnity, fee-for-service plans without third-party review of physician or hospital expenditures. They may also be managed-care plans such as preferred provider organizations, health maintenance organizations, individual practice associations or fee-for-service plans with third-party review. Feldman, Kralewski, and Dowd (1989) have suggested, however, that the distinctions among different forms of plans may be blurred because many plans have varying degrees of freedom of choice of provider, coverage of service, and amount of risk that the provider must bear.

Competition among health plans may be found in many employer groups in both the private and public sectors. As long as there is free entry into the market for health plans, premiums of health plans should be at the competitive level. Even when offering only a single plan, an employer may take competitive bids from insuring organizations to offer the plan with the best combination of premiums and benefits.

Two factors make consumer selection among health plans analogous to the purchase of most goods and services. First, price is a criterion; individuals base their selection of a plan, in part, on the out-of-pocket premiums they will have to pay. For individuals whose employer pays the entire premium, price, of course, will not be a concern.

Second, individuals can make an informed choice in selecting a health care plan. Health plans have incentives to advertise and supply information about themselves to potential customers. Individuals may speak to their firm's benefit counselors to secure additional information. Decisions need not be made immediately; employers usually provide a month in which to decide upon a plan. Moreover, the choice is not irrevocable since individuals usually have the option of switching health plans at least once a year.

The employer may also act as a guarantor of quality for the health care plans it offers. The employer has incentives to retain employees, and one way to do so is to provide attractive health care benefits. If a health benefits plan does not conform to its promises, individuals may have reduced allegiance to the firm. In short, employers (or even unions), in both the private and public sector may, as Enthoven and Kronick (1989a) suggest, act as sponsors in assisting employees to choose among plans. Moreover, competition among insuring organizations, such as competition between alternative delivery systems and fee-for-service plans, may engender more cost consciousness in the fee-for-service plans as they attempt to compete with the alternative delivery systems (see Chapter 5).

Enthoven's consumer-choice health plan

Enthoven's consumer-choice health plan is an important policy prescription for competition among plans. Enthoven makes a number of points in his proposal. First, he envisions competition among "integrated health care systems" such as staff-model health maintenance organizations rather than competition with traditional insurance firms. According to Enthoven, traditional fee-for-service insurance firms will not be able to create incentives to achieve efficiency because providers are not at risk. To assure maximum consumer choice under the Enthoven plan, employers in the private sector would not be able to contribute a greater amount to any single plan they offered.

Second, "sponsors" would play a key role in providing information to enrollees. Sponsors might be employers, unions, state governments (which could have pools of high-risk individuals), and aggregate sponsors of the "unsponsored" small firms that find it unprofitable to offer health insurance on their own to their groups. Finally, sponsors would guard against cream-skimming and inequity in the system by assuring that subsidies are provided to individuals who have high-predicted medical expenses.

Indeed, the insistence on competition among health plans without discrimination against high-risk individuals is an integral part of the Enthoven proposal. Individuals would pay premiums to any plan or receive subsidies based on their actuarial risk. Legislation would require all plans to offer a comprehensive benefits package to all individuals so that plans could not attract only healthy persons by offering reduced-benefit packages. For example, deductibles would not be allowed to exceed $250 per person (Enthoven 1988; Enthoven and Kronick 1989a,b).

Competition among health plans, however, also entails potential complications. Newhouse (1982) suggests that variation would still remain within risk categories and that it would be extremely difficult to eliminate risk selection entirely. For example, risk selection could take place at the physician-patient level if physicians began to treat high-risk patients in a rude manner. Moreover, even if risk selection by health plans were reduced, there would still be the potential problem of adverse selection on the part of the employee. Employees who anticipate high health care expenses may select plans with more comprehensive coverage. This, in turn, will raise the costs and premiums of these plans and lower the costs of plans with reduced coverage (Pauly 1984).

Second, although information may appear to be plentiful on the attributes of the plans, it will be imperfect information. Each plan has many dimensions including its financial relationship with physicians, its quality of care, its cost-containment mechanisms, and its financial viability. If employees err in their choice of health plan, they will find it difficult to remedy before an annual open-enrollment period.

Within this competitive framework (or indeed any framework in which individuals have insurance), individuals still have incentives to consume more health services than would be the case without health insurance. Individuals may consume services in which marginal benefits are nearly zero since there are no direct costs to the patient. Firms may also have to provide these services because of legal liability. In contrast, from society's viewpoint, the optimal allocation of all goods and services occurs when both benefits and costs are considered (Pauly 1979). The differences between an individual's incentives and the achievement of an optimal allocation of resources will be discussed further in Chapter 10.

Competition and the allocation of resources

How might competition in health care affect the allocation of health care resources? There are a number of answers to this question, in part because there is disagreement on what constitutes competition in health care. Reinhardt (1989), for example, defines competition in terms of price competition among providers, suggesting that competition cannot exist if public and private insurance pay for three-quarters of health care bills. Fuchs (1988) also appears to define competition in health care as competition among providers, but he points to the growth of organized health plans as providing additional forms of competition.

Arrow (1968), like Enthoven, focuses on the insurance industry and, therefore, unlike Fuchs and Reinhardt, puts a different emphasis on where competition is most likely to occur. Arrow suggests, for example, that insurance need not completely distort the allocation of health care services. Active cost-conscious insurers, for example, may improve the allocation of resources over what would be the case if the insurers were passive payers.

It appears that, with the increase in the number of HMOs and PPOs and in cost consciousness among insurers (described earlier), some resources have been saved by more vigilant insurer behavior. However, Chapters 10 and 11 will show that even with vigilant insurer behavior there will not be an optimal allocation of resources in the health care sector.

Regulation of price and supply in health care industries, as in other industries, may create inefficiencies and increase price. It may be ineffective insofar as regulated firms may shift costs to unregulated segments. Rather than benefiting the public interest, regulation may benefit the firms that are regulated.

Competition, in contrast, may improve the allocation of resources, but it is not clear that competition will be able to reduce the rate of increase in health care costs. Competition will also do little to reduce any inequities in the provision of health care services.

References

American Medical Care and Review Association (1988). *Preferred Provider Organizations and the Industry Report on PPO Development.*

Arrow, K. J. (1968). "The Economics of Moral Hazard: Further Comment," *American Economic Review* 53: 537–39.

Benham, L. (1972). "The Effect of Advertising on the Price of Eyeglasses," *Journal of Law and Economics* 15: 337–52.

Blair, R., Jackson, J. R., and Vogel, R. (1975). "Economies of Scale in the Administration of Health Insurance," *Review of Economics and Statistics* 57 (no. 2): 185–89.

Brown, C. C. (1988). "Minimum Wage Laws: Are They Overrated," *Journal of Economic Perspectives* 2: 133–45.

Cooper, K., and Fraser, D. R. (1984). *Banking Deregulation and the New Competition in Financial Services.* Cambridge, MA: Ballinger Publishing Co.

Enthoven, A. C. (1988). *Theory and Practice of Managed Competition in Health Care Finance.* Netherlands: Elsevier Science Publishing Company.

Enthoven, A., and Kronick, R. (1989a). "A Consumer-Choice Health Plan for the 1990's," (First of two parts) *New England Journal of Medicine* 320 (no. 2): 29–37.

———. (1989b). "A Consumer-Choice Health Plan for the 1990's," (Second of two parts) *The New England Journal of Medicine* 320: 94–101.

Fanara, P., Jr., and Greenberg, W. (1985). "Factors Affecting the Adoption of Prospective Reimbursement Programs by State Governments." In *Incentives v. Controls in Health Policy,* ed. J. A. Meyer, 144–56. American Enterprise Institute.

Feldman, R., and Greenberg, W. (1981). "Blue Cross Market Share, Economies of Scale, and Cost Containment Efforts," *Health Services Research* 16 (no. 2): 175–83.

Feldman, R., Kralewski, J., and Dowd, B. (1989). "Health Maintenance Organizations: The Beginning or the End?" *Health Services Research* 24 (no. 2): 191–211.

Fuchs, V. R. (1988). "The 'Competition Revolution' in Health Care," *Health Affairs* 7: 5–24.

Glaskowsky, N. A. (1986). *Effects of Deregulation on Motor Carriers.* Westport, CT: Eno Foundation on Transportation.

Greenberg, W. (1989). *Response to AIDS in the Private Sector.* Alexandria, VA: Capitol Publications.

Joskow, P. L. (1981). "Alternative Regulatory Mechanisms for Controlling Hospital Costs." In *A New Approach to the Economics of Health Care,* ed. M. Olson, 219–57. Washington, DC: American Enterprise Institute.

Kessel, R. (1958). "Price Discrimination in Medicine," *Journal of Law and Economics* 1: 20–53.

Kwoka, J. E., Jr. (1984). "Advertising and the Price and Quality of Optometric Services," *American Economic Review* 74: 211–16.

Morrisey, M. A., Sloan, F. A., and Valvona, J. (1988). "Defining Geographic Markets for Hospital Care," *Law and Contemporary Problems* 51 (no. 2): 165–94.

Morrison, S., and Winston, C. (1986). *The Economic Effects of Airline Deregulation.* Washington, DC: The Brookings Institution.

Newhouse, J. P. (1982). "Is Competition the Answer?" *Journal of Health Economics* 1: 109–16.

Pauly, M. V. (1984). "Is Cream-Skimming a Problem for the Competitive Medical Market?" *Journal of Health Economics* 3: 87–95.

———. (1978). "Is Medical Care Different?" In *Competition in the Health Care Sector: Past, Present, and Future,* ed. W. Greenberg, 11–35. Germantown, MD: Aspen Publishing.

———. (1979). "What is Unnecessary Surgery?" *Milbank Memorial Fund Quarterly/Health and Society* 57 (no. 1): 95–116.

Peltzman, S. (1976). "Toward a More General Theory of Regulation," *The Journal of Law and Economics* 19 (no. 2): 211–40.

Reinhardt, U. E. (1989). "Economists in Health Care: Saviors or Elephants in a Porcelain Shop?" *American Economic Review* 79 (no. 2): 337–42.

Salkever, D. C. and Bice, T. W. (1976). "The Impact of Certificate-of-Need Controls on Hospital Investment," *Milbank Memorial Fund Quarterly* 54: 195–214.

Shortell, S. M., and Hughes, E. F. X. (1988). "The Effects of Regulation Competition and Ownership on Mortality Rates among Hospital Inpatients," *New England Journal of Medicine* 318 (no. 17): 1100–07.

Sloan, F. A. (1983). "Rate Regulation as a Strategy for Cost Control: Evidence from the Last Decade," *Milbank Memorial Fund Quarterly* 61: 195–217.

Stigler, G. J. (1971). "The Theory of Economic Regulation," *Bell Journal of Economics and Management Science* 2 (no. 1): 3–21.

Summers, L. H. (1989). "Some Simple Economics of Mandated Benefits," *American Economic Review* 79: 177–83.

Weller, C. D. (1984). "'Free Choice' as a Restraint of Trade in American Health Care Delivery and Insurance," *Iowa Law Review* 69: 1351–94.

Williams, A. P., Schwartz, W. B., Newhouse, J. P., and Bennett, B. W. (1983). "How Many Miles to the Doctor?" *New England Journal of Medicine* 309 (no. 16): 958–63.

8

Antitrust in the Health Care Sector

The aim of the nation's antitrust laws is to promote competition within industries. Economic theory suggests that the greater the number of firms within an industry and the fewer the impediments to firms that would like to enter that industry, the more competitive the industry will be. Moreover, the behavior of firms within industries may indicate the extent of competition. For example, price collusion among firms indicates a lack of competition in an industry. Exclusion of new entrants by firms that are already in the industry may also be anticompetitive in that it reduces the number of potential competitors.

Antitrust legislation is essential to a competitive environment in health care. The first antitrust law, the Sherman Act, however, was enacted in 1890 as a response to the oil and tobacco trusts. These industries were believed to have fewer firms and higher prices than would have been the case if anticompetitive behavior, such as predatory pricing or price fixing, were prohibited.

Under Section 1 of the Sherman Act, "[E]very contract, combination in the form of trust or otherwise, or conspiracy, in restraint of trade or commerce . . . is illegal." Section 2 of the Act states that "[E]very person who shall monopolize, or attempt to monopolize, or combine or conspire with any other person or persons, to monopolize any part of the trade or commerce . . . shall be deemed guilty. . . ."

Two additional major antitrust laws have been passed since the Sherman Act. Major provisions of the Clayton Act, passed in 1914, were intended to prohibit price discrimination in which sellers "discriminate in price between different purchasers of commodities of like grade and quality" (Section 2) and to eliminate mergers that "lessen competition or tend to create a monopoly" (Section 7). Price discrimination (charging lower prices to larger buyers) was alleged to give larger buyers an unfair advantage over smaller buyers. In addition, anticompetitive mergers might reduce the number of competitors, thereby lessening competition and creating a monopoly.

The Federal Trade Commission Act was also passed in 1914. Section 5 of this act forbade "unfair methods of competition" and created a new agency, the Federal Trade Commission, to help enforce the antitrust laws. Antitrust suits may be brought both by the Federal Trade Commission and by the U.S. Department of Justice, although only the Justice Department can bring suits that involve Sherman Act violations in criminal proceedings. Private plaintiffs and state antitrust authorities may also bring antitrust suits, although these suits tend to be of lesser importance.

Consistent with the notion of a competitive health care system is the proposition that an increase in the supply of sellers will not only bring lower prices to consumers but improve consumer welfare. It is expected that an increased number of these sellers, such as physicians or hospitals, will bring a more efficient allocation of resources, improved quality of care, greater innovation and technology, greater access to providers, and a greater variety of services for consumers. This expected result of increased supply is not unlike the expectations in other sectors of the economy when antitrust actions are brought.

An increased supply of providers is directly antithetical to a health care regulatory environment that emphasizes limiting the number of beds or number of hospitals. For example, in many states with certificate-of-need laws, planning agencies have attempted to restrict the number of new hospital beds or have reduced the number of already existing beds.

Crucial to the assumption that an increased number of competitors improves the welfare of consumers is the presence of knowledgeable buyers and demanders of goods and services, that is, a belief in the notion of consumer sovereignty is a requisite to the proposition that antitrust has a role to play in the health care sector. Demand in the health care sector arises, however, mostly from third-party payers, not individual patients. Antitrust policy is therefore directed toward ensuring that third-party payers can act as prudent buyers in the purchase of health care without boycotts or interference from providers. For services that are uninsured, individuals are expected to compare prices and the quality of providers as they would for any other good or service.

Information on the quality and price of services offered by health care providers is fundamental to an effective antitrust policy if third parties and individuals are to act as informed buyers. To the extent that physicians can create their own demand because of uninformed buyers or patients cannot assess the relative quality of medical and nonmedical providers, antitrust laws will be less effective.

Legal and Economic Impediments to Antitrust Policy in the Health Care Sector

Until 1975, due to legal impediments and a number of economic factors, there were few antitrust suits brought in the health care sector. Perhaps the most important legal obstacle was the belief that the health care professions were exempt from antitrust legislation because of their status as "learned professions." In *Goldfarb v. Virginia State Bar,* 421 US 773 (1975), however, the court found that the learned professions were not exempt from antitrust scrutiny. In this case, the Supreme Court found that the Virginia state bar association was in violation of Section 1 of the Sherman Act for setting minimum fee schedules.

A second obstacle to antitrust enforcement was the McCarran-Ferguson Act, which was referred to in Chapter 7. The presence of the commercial insurers, Blue Cross, and alternative delivery systems, such as health maintenance organizations, made it questionable whether the antitrust laws would be applicable to such firms. Gradually, however, the courts interpreted the McCarran-Ferguson Act to apply only to the actual business of insurance such as the underwriting of risks rather than to insurance firms and their relationships to health care providers.

Finally, many health care organizations, such as most hospitals, Blue Cross and Blue Shield insurance plans, and some nursing homes, are nonprofit firms. Section 4 of the Federal Trade Commission Act limits Federal Trade Commission jurisdiction to the corporation "organized to carry on business for its own profit or that of its members," although the Justice Department is not prohibited from bringing antitrust suits against nonprofit firms. Moreover, the Federal Trade Commission has suggested that nonprofit organizations can indirectly benefit for-profit providers with whom they are affiliated. For example, in a staff report, the Bureau of Economics of the Federal Trade Commission (1979) argued that the nonprofit Blue Shield plan existed for the benefit of the profit-making physicians on its board. Subsequent to this report, all Blue Shield plans voluntarily eliminated physician-controlled boards.

In addition to legal barriers, economic considerations contributed to the low level of antitrust activity in health care. A relatively scarce supply of physicians, until the 1970s, made it less likely, for example, that hospitals would deny staff privileges to physicians. On the demand side, third-party payers, until the early 1980s, usually paid the bill for health care providers' services without much concern about the cost of the services or number of services performed. Third-party payers, in short, were not prudent buyers; there was little reason for providers to resist third-party payment mechanisms.

Antitrust litigation in health care may be divided between cases that have attempted to affect supply, by increasing the variety and number of providers, and cases that have affected demand, by enabling third parties to be more prudent buyers. The following discussion examines first the supply-side cases and then the demand-side cases. Taken sequentially, these cases illustrate the role of antitrust in the supply of information; the supply of alternative delivery systems; the supply of nonphysician providers; the supply of physician providers; the supply of hospitals; and the attempts of third-party payers to control provider utilization and to contain provider fees.

The Supply Side

Antitrust and an increase in supply

AMA v. US, 317 US 519 (1943), involved an attempt by physicians to restrict the entry of a health maintenance organization, Group Health Association, into the Washington, D.C., area. Physicians who elected to work for Group Health Association were denied hospital staff privileges, isolated from the medical society, and subjected to verbal abuse and peer pressure from area physicians. The Supreme Court found that the American Medical Association and the local medical society were guilty of concerted criminal action in violation of Section 1 of the Sherman Act and ordered them to cease coercing physicians who wanted to work for Group Health Association. By 1987, Group Health Association had more than 140,000 members—members who would have been denied their choice of HMO membership if the local medical society and the American Medical Association had prevailed four decades earlier.

The *Goldfarb* decision, which subjected the learned professions to the antitrust laws, ushered in the current generation of antitrust litigation. An important objective of *Federal Trade Commission v. American Medical Association,* 94 FTC 701 (1979), aff'd 638 F. 2d 443 (2d Cir. 1980), aff'd 452 US 960 (1982), one of the first cases brought after *Goldfarb,* was to attempt to increase the supply of information in the marketplace. Economists have always considered information to be an essential good, or commodity, in the marketplace. In health care, as in other sectors providing goods and services, consumers or third parties with an increased supply of information can reduce the costs of search for the particular price or quality of service they desire. Increased information may also create more competition as the providers compete on the basis of price and quality.

In *Federal Trade Commission v. American Medical Association* it was alleged that the American Medical Association inhibited the supply of information from physicians by making various forms of information dissemination a violation of the AMA code of ethics, which prohibited the solicitation of patients. (The American Dental Association had a similar prohibition on advertising by dentists.) In May 1982, the Supreme Court affirmed the Court of Appeals ruling that the American Medical Association violated Section 5 of the Federal Trade Commission Act.

Supply of alternative delivery systems

In the same suit against the American Medical Association, the FTC alleged that the AMA inhibited the growth of contract practice medicine, an arrangement that enabled a group of physicians to contract with a private payer of health services, such as a preferred provider organization or a health maintenance organization, which would then compete against physicians who were not members of the group. After the Supreme Court decision, the AMA code of ethics could no longer prohibit contract medicine. As a consequence, more than 600 preferred provider organizations with more than 32 million enrollees had been formed by 1987.

There are also a number of federal antitrust actions that have prevented physicians from hindering the growth of health maintenance organizations. The growth of health maintenance organizations or alternative delivery systems is consistent with a competitive framework for a number of reasons. First, alternative delivery systems are additional competitors in the marketplace, increasing the scope of consumer choice. Second, health maintenance organizations may engender competition in the fee-for-service sector, which may put downward pressure on hospitalization rates in that sector. HMOs, for example, may compete directly with Blue Cross so that the latter may reduce hospital utilization and increase benefit packages in response to the competition.

Two early antitrust cases involved physicians in fee-for-service medicine who interfered with HMO growth. The first, *FTC v. Medical Service Corporation of Spokane County*, 88 FTC 906, (1976), involved an FTC complaint against the Medical Service Corporation, a Blue Shield plan, for interfering with the growth of HMOs in the eastern portion of the state of Washington. Physicians were not allowed to become participating members of the state's Blue Shield plan if they worked for an HMO. Since the Blue Shield plan was the largest insurer in its region, this was a significant sanction against HMO physicians. In a consent order, Medical Service Corporation of Spokane County agreed not to discriminate against HMO-based physicians. (A consent order, which provides for some remedial action but does not determine guilt or innocence, is not uncommon in antitrust cases.)

In a closely related case, *FTC v. Forbes Health System Medical Staff*, 94 FTC 1042 (1979), the Federal Trade Commission filed suit against the Forbes Health System medical staff in Pittsburgh, which prevented physicians who affiliated with HMOs from obtaining hospital staff privileges. Without access to hospitals, many physicians could not practice medicine. In the consent order, the Forbes Health System physicians had to refrain from discriminating against physicians who elected to join HMOs.

The effect of both of these cases was to allow HMOs to compete in the marketplace based on their own merits. The Federal Trade Commission had not endorsed HMOs; rather, it provided the opportunity for consumers to choose among health plans.

More recently the Federal Trade Commission brought a case against the medical staff of Doctors' Hospital (*FTC v. Medical Staff of Doctors' Hospital of Prince George's County*, File No. C–3226 settled by Consent Agreement, April 14, 1988) for conspiring to prevent George Washington University (GWU) Health Plan from opening a satellite facility in Prince George's County, Maryland. George Washington University Health Plan, an established HMO in Washington, D.C., had an enrollment of more than 25,000 individuals in 1987 and had opened a number of satellite clinics in the Washington metropolitan area. According to the FTC complaint, the medical staff of Doctors' Hospital threatened to close the hospital, which would make it difficult for GWU Health Plan to become established in that area. In the consent order reached with the FTC, the medical staff of Doctor's Hospital agreed not to prevent GWU Health Plan from opening a branch in Prince George's County.

Courts have not always ruled in favor of competition or the consumer in cases involving the formation of health maintenance organizations or preferred provider organizations. For instance, in *Arizona v. Maricopa County Medical Society*, 457 US 332 (1982), the U.S. Supreme Court ruled in a four-to-three decision that the Maricopa Foundation for Medical Care, a nonprofit Arizona corporation, had violated Section 1 of the Sherman Act by engaging in the fixing of maximum prices.

Approximately 1,750 physicians, or 70 percent, of the county's private physicians belonged to the Maricopa Foundation. Each of the physicians agreed to a maximum fee for his or her services. In addition, the foundation reviewed physician treatments for medical necessity. Physicians who hospitalized patients had their diagnoses and prescribed lengths of stay reviewed prior to their patients' admissions.

A 70 percent market share by a single entity in a marketplace might be of antitrust concern because of the potential for the abuse of market power. However, a significant market share is only harmful when there are barriers to entry into the marketplace. If new firms can enter the market, monopoly profits earned by the firm with the large market share can be dissipated. In *Maricopa*, there did not appear to be barriers to physicians entering the Arizona market. For example, market shares of HMOs in Arizona and in Phoenix (the center of Maricopa County) grew dramatically just prior to the antitrust suit. In addition, there were a large number of commercial insurers in the market.

The Supreme Court ruled that the Maricopa Foundation was illegal because of its price-fixing activities. Price fixing per se had been found to be illegal in a series of earlier Supreme Court decisions, yet this was maximum price fixing. Physicians could set prices lower than the maximum if the demand for their services warranted a lower price. Moreover, the Maricopa Foundation may have been a procompetitive force in the marketplace, especially when it competed with other fee-for-service plans.

Supply of nonphysician providers

At the individual provider level also, the antitrust authorities have sought to inject more competition into the marketplace. To encourage this competition, the Federal Trade Commission has attempted to eliminate restraints on the practice of medicine by nonphysician providers. In *FTC v. State Volunteer Mutual Insurance Corporation*, 102 FTC 1232 (1983), a physician-sponsored insurance plan in Tennessee allegedly would not provide malpractice insurance to physicians who worked with self-employed nurse-midwives. The plan would insure only those physicians who directly employed nurse-midwives. If nurse-midwives were self-employed, there would be more competition (including low-cost competition) from these nonphysician providers. In 1983, the Federal Trade Commission obtained a consent order from the State Volunteer Mutual Insurance Corporation forbidding it to discriminate against physicians who supervised self-employed nurse-midwives.

Some physicians have attempted to limit the ability of chiropractors, psychologists, and osteopaths to compete with persons who have medical doctor (M.D.) degrees. In *Wilk v. American Medical Association*, 895 F.2d 352 (1990), for example, the American Medical Association, a number of specialty medical associations, and a number of physicians were accused of refusing to deal professionally with chiropractors and of questioning chiropractors' ability to perform certain services. In addition, some physician groups refused to accept referrals from chiropractors or would deny chiropractors access to hospital staffs and hospital diagnostic services. The Seventh Circuit Court found the American Medical Association to be in violation of Section 1 of the Sherman Act.

In *Virginia Academy of Clinical Psychologists v. Blue Shield of Virginia*, 624 F.2d 476 (1980), the two defendent Blue Shield plans denied payment to psychologists unless the psychologists billed their patients through a physician. Blue Shield plans were controlled by physicians and by refusing to pay psychologists except in combination with physicians, plans were thwarting competition between the two groups. The fact that a majority of the boards of directors of Blue Shield were physicians and the fact that psychologists and psychiatrists compete were crucial to the Court of Appeals decision against the physician-controlled Blue Shield plans.

In *Weiss v. York*, 745 F. 2d 786 (1984), osteopathic physicians in York, Pennsylvania, brought suit against York Hospital for violating Sherman Act Sections 1 and 2 by discriminating against osteopathic physicians in awarding staff privileges. The Court's decision in favor of the plaintiff was based, in part, on the fact that an entire class of providers was discriminated against. Moreover, the Court believed that osteopaths, if allowed hospital staff privileges, would generate significant competition for physicians.

In each of these suits, the Court ruled in favor of the plaintiff or the Federal Trade Commission obtained a favorable consent order. In the same way that antitrust rulings improved the variety and number of alternative delivery systems, these rulings improved the variety and number of allied health professionals.

Supply of physicians

If physicians can bar competitors from the marketplace, physicians may be able to realize higher incomes. One way to exclude competitors is to impose restrictions on staff privileges at hospitals. Physicians may be employed at hospitals or they may have their own offices and admit patients to hospitals through their staff admitting privileges. On the other hand, physicians and the hospitals with which they are associated may believe that they can compete more effectively against other hospitals if they can be influential in selecting their own prospective colleagues.

In *Robinson v. Magovern*, 521 F. Supp. 842 (1981), aff'd mem. 688 F. 2d 824 3d Cir. (1982), cardiac surgeon Robinson was denied privileges on the staff of Allegheny General Hospital because surgeon Magovern and the other physicians on the staff of the hospital believed that Robinson had neither the interest in research nor the personality to be acceptable to the hospital. If Robinson were accepted as one of the cardiac surgeons, the hospital would be acting procompetitively since it would increase the number of physicians among whom patients could select. However, the executive committee and Allegheny General Hospital argued that Robinson would not be acceptable to the hospital because he would not concentrate all of his practice at Allegheny General and might not be able to "function harmoniously with the medical staff, the residents, and the support personnel," 521 F. Supp. 875.

The Court ruled that a hospital must be able to select the surgeons with whom it can best compete in the marketplace. Moreover, according to the Court, Allegheny General Hospital does not have a monopoly in the relevant Pittsburgh areas. If the hospital, to the benefit of its existing staff, were to raise its prices much above other hospitals, patients and insurers might increasingly use other hospitals in Pittsburgh. Moreover, the confirmation of Allegheny's prerogative of refusing privileges to Robinson suggests that hospitals and staff physicians can continue to compete on the basis of their perception of a quality-oriented medical staff.

In *Jefferson Parish Hospital v. Hyde*, 466 US 2 (1984), the hospital had an exclusive contract with its anesthesiologists. One anesthesiologist, Hyde, sued the hospital, suggesting that exclusive contracts are anticompetitive. In addition, Hyde complained that an anticompetitive tying arrangement existed between the hospital and the anesthesiologists such that a patient who had surgery at the hospital had no choice but to use the hospital's anesthesiologists. The Court suggested, however, that the hospital did not have monopoly power since it was competing against other hospitals in the area. Moreover, if the physicians under the exclusive contract attempted to capture additional profits, they could be replaced at the expiration of their contract by a new group of physicians. Similar to the *Robinson v. Magovern* case, it was believed that a hospital's right to determine the sorts of physicians with which it contracts in a competitive marketplace outweighs any potential restrictions on competition.

Finally, *Patrick v. Burget,* 486 US 94 (1988), reveals most vividly the potential conflict between the interests of physicians in determining the staff of the hospital in which they are associated and society's interest in maintaining or increasing the number of competitors. In Astoria, Oregon, a physician, Patrick, was denied referrals and dismissed from the city's only hospital, Columbia Memorial Hospital, because of practicing poor-quality care, according to physicians on the hospital's quality review committee. Patrick denied these claims, suggesting that he was dismissed because he had set up his own surgical practice; his practice competed directly with the Astoria Clinic staffed by his colleagues at the hospital who had conspired to eliminate him as a competitor. Although the defendants had won in the Court of Appeals, the Supreme Court decided in Dr. Patrick's favor, suggesting that peer review committees that examine quality are not automatically immune from antitrust litigation.

In *Patrick v. Burget,* the degree of quality of physician care was determined for all the physicians in Astoria by the hospital's quality review committee. There was little choice for the community but to abide by the judgment of the reviewing physicians in their definition of quality. It appears that a particularly strong case would have had to be made that the proficiency of a competing physician was clearly inferior since a competitor was to have been eliminated from the only hospital in the city. After the *Patrick v. Burget* decision, hospital peer review committees were not absolutely immune from potential antitrust litigation by physicians who might be excluded from the marketplace.

Physicians have attempted to raise barriers to entry to physicians who might want to practice in certain geographic markets. In *FTC v. J. Thomas Arno, M.D. et al.*, 109 FTC 61 (1987), a group of physicians in Crawford County, Pennsylvania, near the city of Meadville, allegedly attempted to keep a group of physician specialists located in Erie, Pennsylvania, a nearby city, from establishing a multispecialty medical office in Meadville. The respondents allegedly conspired to prevent or delay the establishment of the new medical office by jointly threatening to cease referring patients to the Erie group establishing the office. In the consent agreement with the Federal Trade Commission, the respondents agreed not to refuse to deal with or withhold patient referrals from any physician or group of physicians if the effect would be to impede competition unreasonably.

Physicians have also attempted to block the entry of physicians who desired to begin a new health care facility. Plaintiffs in *FTC v. Medical Staff of John C. Lincoln Hospital and Health Center*, 106 FTC 291 (1985), alleged that the medical staff of Lincoln Hospital in Phoenix, Arizona, conspired to coerce and threaten to boycott Lincoln Hospital because of the hospital's plan to open an urgent care center within three miles of the hospital. As an outpatient facility, the urgent care center might have resulted in lower costs, creating additional competition for the physicians and the hospital. In the consent agreement, respondent physicians agreed, among other things, not to "make any express or implied threat of any unreasonably discriminatory action against a health care facility, institution, or professional."

Supply of hospitals

Horizontal mergers are mergers between firms in the same industry. The effect of these mergers is to reduce the number of competitors, thereby potentially making an industry less competitive. If there are high barriers to entry to the industry, the anticompetitive effects may be particularly severe. Conversely, if entry to an industry is easy, new firms may undercut the merged firms' higher prices. Horizontal mergers may create efficiencies or economies of scale, enabling the merged firms to reduce average total costs by spreading out the fixed costs of management, technology, and equipment. Thus, horizontal mergers, in reducing the number of firms in an industry, have the potential to increase concentration and raise prices or to make greater economies possible and lower costs and prices.

It is necessary to define the relevant economic market in order to determine whether or not a merger may be anticompetitive. The relevant market is based on both product and geographic considerations. A hospital market may include all of a hospital's services, inpatient services only, or a particular service such as gynecological care. A teaching hospital may or may not provide the same output as a community hospital. Economists have often used the degree of cross-elasticity of demand as one measure of what constitutes a relevant economic market. Cross-elasticity of demand is defined as the relative change in demand for commodity A in response to a relative change in price of commodity B. A high cross-elasticity of demand may indicate that products might be substitutable and, therefore, in the same relevant market. For example, if hospital B raises its price and a large number of patients switch to hospital A, the two hospitals might be considered to be in the same relevant market. Even if products are not currently in the same market, there can be potential competition because firms may be able to enter a particular market with little difficulty. For example, if the ambulatory care unit of a hospital is the relevant market, many hospitals might be able to add such units with little difficulty, thereby increasing the scope of the relevant market.

The extent of the geographic market may, of course, vary by type of service. The size of the relevant hospital market may be greater for more risky procedures like open-heart surgery, for which individuals may consider a large number of hospitals over a greater geographic distance, than for procedures like appendectomies, for which local hospitals may suffice.

In 1979, American Medical International acquired a competing hospital, French Hospital, in San Luis Obispo, California. The Federal Trade Commission, 107 FTC 310 (1984), maintained that the acquisition violated Section 7 of the Clayton Act by eliminating a competitor from the marketplace and increasing the concentration of hospital services in San Luis Obispo and San Luis Obispo County. Both the full commission and the FTC administrative law judge agreed with the commission complaint. Subsequent to the decision, American Medical International had to sell the hospital to another purchaser.

In another hospital merger challenged by the Federal Trade Commission, 106 FTC 361 (1985), aff'd 807 F. 2d 1381 (7th Cir. 1986), cert. denied, 197 S.Ct. 1975 (1987), Hospital Corporation of America purchased the Hospital Affiliates International chain of hospitals as well as the Health Care Corporation chain. The relevant geographic market in which these chains owned or contract-managed hospitals was defined as the Chattanooga, Tennessee, area. A wider geographic area was rejected by the U.S. Court of Appeals when it suggested that patients do not leave the city for hospital emergencies, while for hospital visits in general, physicians are reluctant to send patients where they do not have staff privileges. The Court acknowledged that hospitals might compete with nonhospital providers but suggested that this would not be the rule for the bulk of hospital services.

When the relevant market was defined as only those hospitals in Chattanooga, Hospital Corporation of America was found to own or manage five of the eleven hospitals in the city and 26 percent of hospital services in what the Court described as a highly concentrated market. The Court found Hospital Corporation of America to be in violation of Section 7 of the Clayton Act and ordered the company to divest itself of two hospitals and to terminate its management contract with a third hospital. By insisting on divestiture of the two hospitals, the Federal Trade Commission returned the hospital market to its pre-merger status quo. No additional competitors were created. However, without FTC action, there would have been fewer firms in the market. This reduction in supply might have resulted in increases in prices to patients and third parties.

The Demand Side

As we have seen in Chapter 2, economists have had an ongoing debate about whether an increase in the number of providers may be reflected in an increase in prices or an increase in number of services rendered. One aspect of this debate is whether physicians can create their own demand or set their own price, or whether hospitals may be filled with unnecessary admissions.

This debate arises because of the possible asymmetry of information between the provider and the consumer of medical care. Providers are the experts in medical care, whereas patients generally lack information on the types of procedures and tests to be used. Third-party payers, however, have the ability to monitor providers because of the data they accumulate from insuring large numbers of patients. It is essential for cost containment, therefore, that third-party payers (1) secure information from providers on utilization and prices and (2) be able to contain costs without hindrance by providers.

A 1930s case brought by the U.S. Department of Justice, *U.S. v. Oregon State Medical Society*, 343 US 326 (1952), shows the early importance of utilization review by third-party insurers in their attempts to contain costs. In that case, insurers monitored the decisions of physicians to hospitalize patients, to extend the length of the hospital stay, and to determine which tests were to be performed. Physicians, however, began to resist reviews by the third-party payers. Physicians began their own health insurance plan, Oregon Physicians' Service (OPS), the forerunner to the current Blue Shield plan in Oregon, in an attempt to control utilization-review efforts by other third-party insurers. After the formation of OPS, physicians refused reimbursement by other third-party insurers since they could always rely on reimbursement by

OPS. The cost-containing activities of the insurers were subsequently eliminated.

The Justice Department brought suit against the Oregon State Medical Society, eight county medical societies, and eight physicians for violating Sections 1 and 2 of the Sherman Act by attempting to exclude the insurers that were performing cost containment from the market. Since the three largest private insurers had not been excluded, and no overt action by providers to boycott insurers was found, the Supreme Court ruled seven-to-one in 1952 that the Oregon State Medical Society had not engaged in anticompetitive behavior. The ability of the physicians to thwart utilization-review attempts by insurers discouraged utilization review by third parties for decades. Subsequent boycotts by provider groups were, however, found to be in violation of the antitrust laws.

The Federal Trade Commission brought suits against the Indiana Dental Association, 93 FTC 392 (1979), and the Indiana Federation of Dentists, 101 FTC 57 (1983), rev'd 745 F.2d 1124 (7th Cir. 1984), rev'd 476 US 447 (1986), because the dentists in Indiana refused to furnish x-rays to third-party payers, such as Aetna and Prudential, who desired to contain costs. In dentistry, unlike most of medicine, there can be a time lag between diagnosis and when a procedure must be performed. Dental insurers, therefore, may require x-rays before authorizing treatment and then, with consulting dentists on their staffs, may disapprove payment for some of the dental procedures. In Indiana, however, dentists collectively declined to comply with the x-ray requirement. The Texas Dental Association, 100 FTC 536 (1982), also hindered third-party payers from their cost-containment programs when, together with its members, it refused to furnish x-rays and other diagnostic information to third-party payers.

Both the Indiana Dental Association and the Texas Dental Association agreed in consent orders with the Federal Trade Commission not to obstruct third-party cost-containment efforts or to coerce insurers into using association-approved independent dental consultants. *FTC v. Indiana Federation of Dentists* was eventually decided by the U.S. Supreme Court, which found that the conspiracy to withhold x-rays was in restraint of trade. The Federation's arguments that insurers interfered in the dentist-patient relationship and curtailed professional prerogatives were not persuasive to the Court.

In addition to cases that involve third-party attempts to review utilization, there have also been attempts by third parties to contain the fees of providers. In 1979, the Federal Trade Commission brought suit against the Michigan State Medical Society, 101 FTC 191 (1983), which had allegedly interfered with the reimbursement policies of the commercial insurers, Blue Shield of Michigan, and the state Medicaid authorities. The Commission ruled that the boycott of the insuring organizations by the medical society had the effect of decreasing competition among insuring organizations, with the result of higher fees to patients. In the consent order, the Michigan State Medical Society was no longer allowed to coerce third-party payers into accepting the cost-containment terms it dictated.

Finally, in a private antitrust action, *Kartell v. Blue Shield of Massachusetts, Inc.*, 749 F.2d 922 (1984), Blue Shield, which enrolled more than 50 percent of the Massachusetts population, was sued by Kartell, a physician, on behalf of fellow physicians, because of Blue Shield's stringent reimbursement policies. Blue Shield would not allow physicians to increase their revenues by charging their patients a fee in addition to the fee paid by Blue Shield. The Court of Appeals found that Blue Shield was not in violation of the Sherman Act and should be able to pay what it considered to be a market price for physician services in order to compete. That is, Blue Shield was exercising its right as a prudent buyer.

This group of cases from the demand side illustrates how antitrust policy can alter the demand for health care. Since insurance coverage usually means an increased demand for health care (the demand curve is shifted upward to the right), a prudent buyer may be able to shift the demand curve to the left. This downward shift in the demand curve may reduce the potential increase in utilization occasioned by the presence of insurance.

Antitrust in the Health Care Sector: An Evaluation

It appears that the courts and the Federal Trade Commission have ruled in favor of more rather than less competition in the health care sector. The rulings suggest a desire to have a greater number of physician substitutes competing with physicians, a preference for more physicians competing against one another, and a preference for more competition among hospitals. In cases involving staff privileges at hospitals, the courts, except for *Patrick v. Burget*, allowed existing staff arrangements to continue unless an entire class of providers was denied privileges. In each of the demand-side cases, the courts allowed the third party, as prudent buyer, to attempt to contain costs and ruled against physician or dentist boycotts of third-party payers.

The courts appear to have applied the antitrust laws in health care as they would have applied these laws in any other sector, assuming that competition rather than planning or regulation would curb excessive costs as well as improve quality. Those who believe that the health care sector has peculiar properties that other sectors do not have might disagree with these attempts to make health care industries more competitive. However, each industry is unique, and antitrust would be irrelevant if each industry were to attempt to secure an exemption from litigation on the grounds that that industry was somehow different from other industries in the economy.

Antitrust appears to be as important to a competitive policy in health care as it is in any other sector. A competitive policy can make an industry more efficient and in health care, absent any rightward shift in demand, can contribute to a reduction in costs. Without antitrust, it would not be difficult to imagine health care dominated by the higher-priced physicians (without the choice of lower-priced nonphysician providers) and without any controls on prices and costs by third-party payers. One might also predict a larger number of horizontal mergers, which would increase concentration.

The health care marketplace as a whole has become more competitive since the *Goldfarb* decision in 1975. There has been substantial growth in a variety of alternative delivery systems, growth that might have been slowed considerably if physicians had been allowed to interfere with it. Antitrust may also have improved access to care because of a greater number of providers in the marketplace. Moreover, antitrust may have had deterrent effects on anticompetitive behavior. Litigation costs in antitrust cases can be substantial. Firms found in violation of the Sherman Act may be fined an amount equal to three times the damages of the antitrust action.

In the future, antitrust litigation may play an even larger role in the health care sector. An increasing number of physicians being graduated from medical school, an increasing number of excess beds, and an increasing aggressiveness among nonphysician providers, within tightened private- and public-sector budgets, all point to increased antitrust activity as providers compete for a shrinking per capita reimbursement.

Reference

U.S. Federal Trade Commission, Bureau of Economics (1979). *Staff Report on Physician Control of Blue Shield Plans.* Washington, DC: U.S. Government Printing Office.

9

Long-Term Care

Long-term care consists of health care services, social services, and residential services provided to disabled or elderly persons for a long period of time. Long-term care expenditures have been the fastest-growing portion of the health care sector. Between 1980 and 1988, for example, nursing home expenditures more than doubled from $20.0 billion to $43.1 billion, and nonfacility-based home health care—which includes preventive, supportive, therapeutic, or rehabilitative services—grew even faster (from $1.3 billion to $4.4 billion between 1980 and 1988) (Health Care Financing Administration 1990). Holahan and Cohen's (1987) more precise breakout of Medicaid long-term care expenditures finds that in 1984, 95 percent were reimbursements for institutional care (in nursing homes, intermediate care facilities for the mentally retarded, and mental hospitals), and the rest were for home health care. Moreover, as Bishop (1988) points out, more than 70 percent of individuals who need long-term care assistance live in their own homes and receive most of their aid from family and friends.

The long-term care industry should grow even faster in the future since those over the age of 65 are the fastest-growing segment of the U.S. population. Moreover, the fastest-growing portion of the 65-and-older group is the oldest segment—people over the age of 85. In 1985, there were approximately 29 million individuals over the age of 65 and 2.7 million individuals over the age of 85, or 12.0 and 1.1 percent of the population, respectively. By the year 2030, there will be approximately 65 million individuals over the age of 65 and approximately 9 million individuals over the age of 85, or 21.2 percent and 2.8 percent of the population, respectively (*New York Times* 1987). Individuals who are older than 85 are much more likely to need assistance than those between the ages of 65 and 85. Fewer than 40 percent of nursing home residents aged 65 to 74 had difficulty in eating, while approximately 56 percent of residents aged 85 and older needed assistance in eating (Kovar, Hendershot, and Mathis 1989). According to Kovar, Hendershot, and Mathis (1989), about 88 percent of nursing home residents are elderly. The remaining 12 percent are blind, disabled, or retarded.

An increase in the number of elderly individuals and individuals who are very old and disabled will shift the demand curve to the right for long-term care. This upward pressure of demand should increase prices and utilization of long-term care facilities and stimulate investment in new facilities, provided there are no governmental restrictions in pricing or barriers to entry of new and existing firms.

Not all elderly, however, require assistance with daily living activities. Most nursing home residents need assistance with at least one activity of daily living; more than 75 percent, for example, need assistance in bathing (Kovar, Hendershot, and Mathis 1989). Only 7.6 percent of the over-65 population outside nursing homes, however, receives assistance with daily living activities (Kovar, Hendershot, and Mathis 1989).

The mix of competition, regulation, and rationing in order to achieve efficiency, control expenditures, and improve equity is as important in long-term care as it is in acute care. This chapter will compare long-term care with acute care and with other segments of the economy. Next, it will examine more closely the supply side of long-term care, focusing on the structure, conduct, and performance of the nursing home industry. Third, the chapter will analyze the economic effects of Medicaid, Medicare, commercial insurers, and private payers on the supply of long-term care facilities. New long-term care institutions, such as social/health maintenance organizations and continuing care retirement communities (CCRCs), will also be examined. Finally, this chapter will examine the future role of government long-term care policy and the respective roles of the private and public sectors.

Economic Attributes of Long-Term Care

A number of economic attributes make long-term care different from acute care. The first is the limited role of the physician in long-term care. In long-term care, the physician has a passive role; the doctor does not ordinarily have the main responsibility for referring individuals to or placing them in nursing homes or for referring them to home health care agencies. The physician does not usually control the length of stay in nursing homes. Most procedures that require medical attention are performed in hospitals or at ambulatory care facilities rather than in nursing homes. Hence, the curative role of the physician accounts for a very minor proportion of long-term care expenditures. Furthermore, physicians rarely use new technology—which is responsible for so large a proportion of acute care costs—for long-term care purposes.

The second distinctive economic attribute of long-term care is its association with custodial rather than curative care. Long-term care often includes help with such activities as bathing, eating, and dressing. Nursing home stays average more than 600 days, compared to fewer than 7 days in a hospital (Kovar, Hendershot, and Mathis 1989). Once illnesses in hospitals are either cured or stabilized, individuals are allowed to return home. Individuals in long-term care facilities are less likely to return to an environment in which assistance would not be required (although Weissert and Scanlon (1985) report that more than one-quarter of nursing home residents are eventually discharged).

Third, the types and scope of third-party coverage are different for acute and long-term care. In acute care, Medicare and Medicaid together account for approximately 35 percent of expenditures, and private insurance (Blue Cross and Blue Shield and the commercial insurers) accounts for approximately 30 percent. Patients themselves pay about 35 percent of expenditures. In acute care hospitals, public and private insurers cover more than 90 percent of expenditures. In long-term care, however, Medicaid pays approximately 50 percent of expenditures, Medicare and private insurance firms each pay less than 3 percent of expenditures, and individuals pay more than 40 percent with their own funds.

The limited insurance coverage of long-term care services relative to acute care services may reduce the number of procedures and the amount of utilization of long-term care services whose benefits are less than societal cost. However, insured long-term care services, because they usually reduce daily living responsibilities of the elderly, are subject to moral hazard, perhaps to a greater degree than acute care services. Many elderly individuals could justify some assistance in bathing or dressing, for example, if these activities were covered by insurance.

Finally, the determinants of long-term care utilization derive not only from an individual's need for services but also from demographics and the mores of society. A large number of individuals who might have stayed home to care for their parents are now in the formal labor force, which increases the opportunity cost of attending to the needs of elderly parents. In addition, divorce rates have grown, and individuals are unlikely to care for a former spouse's parents. At the same time, families with two working members are now better able to afford professional long-term care services.

Uncertainty and the enormous potential for moral hazard if insurance is obtained to protect oneself from this uncertainty appear to be the major differences between long-term care and other industries. One is uncertain about how long one might live, the degree of one's possible disability, and the future costs of nursing home care and home services. As we shall see, however, individuals are reluctant to purchase long-term care insurance to guard against this uncertainty. Individuals may have a high discount rate such that they place a greater value on current rather than future income. The presence of the Medicaid program, which covers more than 70 percent of nursing home residents, may contribute to this reluctance to purchase private insurance. Moreover, individuals who want to buy insurance may be unable to do so because of its cost or because they are denied coverage due to ill health.

In addition to uncertainty and moral hazard in long-term care, there are information asymmetries between the nursing home and the disabled individual. Although disabled individuals may be able to secure assistance from family and friends in selecting a nursing home, they may have a difficult time (because, for example, of a deteriorating mental state) judging the quality of care provided once they live in one. Moreover, once a person is situated in a nursing home, substantial mental, physical, and financial costs attach to moving that person to another home. For most other goods and services in the economy, there may be information asymmetries between seller and buyer. However, if one buys an inferior automobile or eats in a poor restaurant, at least there is a finite end to the mistake. The selection of an unsuitable nursing home may not be so easily corrected.

There have already been some attempts to provide information in the nursing home market. Nursing homes generally advertise the amenities they offer but rarely advertise the price of their services. In January 1989, the Health Care Financing Administration provided information to the public on nursing homes. In this 75-volume study, information was released on the compliance of 15,000 nursing homes with 32 of 500 federal quality standards. These standards included food preparation and sanitation, patient cleanliness, and administration of drugs. Compliance standards did not reveal the severity of each deficiency, nor were price data revealed in the survey (*Medicine and Health Perspectives* 1989, 1–2).

Competition among Nursing Homes

There were approximately 20,000 nursing homes in the United States in 1985 with an average of 85 beds per home (Kovar, Hendershot, and Mathis 1989). Unlike most hospitals, most nursing homes are for-profit enterprises. Like some hospitals, some nursing homes are owned by religious groups and other nonprofit institutions. More than 40 percent of for-profit as well as nonprofit nursing homes are members of chains (Bishop 1988). Except for certificate-of-need regulations, there do not appear to be barriers to entry to firms that would like to enter the nursing home industry.

Nursing homes compete on the basis of price, quality, and avoidance of higher-risk, older individuals who might consume more services. Firms often use price discrimination in efforts to maximize profits. Since state Medicaid programs only pay at or below the competitive rate, nursing homes usually charge self-pay patients or commercial insurers a higher price. High occupancy rates (generally exceeding 90 percent) have apparently decreased nursing homes' incentive to compete on the basis of quality and to disseminate information on the quality attributes of their homes (Nyman 1989). If excess demand exists, shopping for nursing homes based on quality considerations may not be an option for many Medicaid patients. Firms, therefore, appear to compete on a quality basis only in areas where nursing home occupancy rates are relatively low. Private, self-pay patients who can pay higher prices than Medicaid pays may have a greater choice of nursing homes. Nursing homes have incentives to accept as residents those individuals able to pay prices higher than the prices the homes charge Medicaid patients. Like acute care hospitals, nursing homes also have incentives to admit individuals who, at least at the beginning of their stay, will have less need for costly care.

There are very few studies on the profitability of nursing homes. Vogel (1983), in his review of such studies performed in the 1970s, suggests that there appears to be "large variability" in profit rates among firms. Vogel suggests that higher profit rates may be due to reduced competition in some areas because of certificate-of-need regulations; lower profit rates may also be due to periods of rapid growth of nursing homes in some areas or may be due to the government as a monopsonistic buyer. Nursing homes that have a greater number of self-pay patients may have a higher rate of return, especially if there are certificate-of-need or other requirements to deter new entry. There do not appear to be any economies of scale in the size of nursing homes, however, which might have been able to confer higher-than-competitive rates of return (Bishop 1988).

Medicaid as a Monopsonistic Buyer

Since Medicaid accounts for approximately 50 percent of nursing home expenditures, Medicaid policies can substantially affect the structure, conduct, and performance of the nursing home industry. For example, state Medicaid reimbursement programs that pay a flat per diem fee have experienced a much lower rate of cost increases than those that still pay retrospectively (Holahan 1985). If Medicaid fees are set too low, or if they fail to consider the case mix of nursing home residents and the amount of nursing assistance the residents require, some nursing homes may not survive unless they can raise their fees to private-pay patients.

State approaches to nursing home cost containment have almost always been of a regulatory nature. There has been no competitive bidding as there has been for hospital care in California or for acute care in Arizona. In addition to regulating reimbursement, many states also regulate quality of care. Much quality-of-care regulation is based on the inputs into nursing home care, such as the number of attending nurses or the number of times beds are changed during the week. States also have licensing requirements that are based, in part, on quality considerations.

Certificate-of-need regulation, used by nearly all of the states, has probably had the most profound effect on the nursing home market (Feder and Scanlon 1980). Certificate-of-need laws can be applied either to existing nursing homes that would like to increase their capital expenditures (including an increase in the number of beds) or to new firms that would like to enter the market. Hence, they can create monopoly power and the ability to raise prices above the competitive level for existing firms by artificially reducing the number of available beds. Although the prices nursing homes charge may be regulated by Medicaid, excessive waiting lines and poor quality of care may still result from certificate-of-need laws. For example, costs have been found to be lower in areas of a limited supply of beds, but it appears that this may be due to a reduction in quality rather than to an increase in efficiency (Nyman 1988). A shortage of beds can also intensify cream-skimming among the nursing homes, allowing them to take only those patients who appear to be less costly to care for.

The purported reason for certificate-of-need laws is to control the costs of nursing home care. With fewer beds to be reimbursed, Medicaid would supposedly have lower costs. The potential for reduced costs, however, must be balanced against the potential for reduced quality and reduced access to Medicaid patients as well as the potential for higher prices (due to monopoly power) to non-Medicaid patients. Indeed, Feder and Scanlon (1980) have asked why states have not put greater emphasis on rate-setting policies rather than certificate-of-need laws. It appears that established nursing homes are more comfortable in restricting the supply of beds (and new entrants) rather than tightening nursing home rates.

Private Long-Term Care Insurance

There are, in addition to a number of Blue Cross and Blue Shield plans, approximately 100 commercial insurers that sell private insurance for long-term care. This is a sixfold increase in the number of firms since 1984. Even with the large increase in the number of firms that sell long-term care insurance, however, only slightly more than 1 million policies had been sold as of the end of 1988 (Van Gelder and Johnson 1989).

Most individuals buy long-term care insurance, unlike acute care insurance, on a nongroup basis rather than on an employer-group basis. This increases the transaction costs of selling and marketing insurance as well as the information asymmetries between the seller and buyer of insurance. Only 2 percent of policies sold in 1988 were under employer auspices (Van Gelder and Johnson 1989). Ford Motor Company's recent long-term care policy experiment for approximately 6,600 active and retired employees and their dependents in Louisville, Kentucky, is a notable exception to this trend. Under the Ford policy, nursing home or home health care benefits will be provided to those who are severely impaired and are in need of custodial care (*New York Times* 1989, D-20).

In a survey of 30 commercial firms, the Health Insurance Association of America found that many of the plans provided for coverage of skilled and intermediate nursing home care as well as for home health care. Similar to much of the acute care sector, all of the policies sold by the firms had preexisting condition clauses to curb the enrollment of high-risk individuals (Van Gelder and Johnson 1989).

Why has private insurance for long-term care not grown as fast as acute care coverage, especially group insurance offered by employers?

There may be a number of reasons. First, individuals may have a high discount rate such that they place a greater value on current rather than future income. Second, the presence of the Medicaid program, which covers more than 70 percent of individuals in nursing homes, may contribute to a reluctance to purchase private insurance. Some individuals may look upon Medicaid as a safety net for long-term care in case they do not have sufficient funds or insurance in their old age. In a survey undertaken by the Health Insurance Association of America, more than 16 percent of the respondents believed that the government would be available to pay $2,000 a month if nursing home care were needed (Meiners 1989). Economists have suggested that, in the same way, the prospect of Social Security income in one's old age may have deterred American savings.

Third, those most interested in buying long-term care insurance may be excluded by preexisting conditions or may find the premiums for those buyers near retirement age to be prohibitively expensive. In contrast, younger individuals may not be interested in purchasing insurance unlikely to benefit them for as much as 20 to 40 years in the future.

Alternatives to Nursing Homes in Long-Term Care

Capitated, comprehensive health care plans are a growing segment of long-term care as they are in acute care. The long-term care plans may vary from continuing care retirement communities to social/health maintenance organizations. Like acute care, comprehensive care takes many forms, of which CCRCs and S/HMOs are prominent examples. In both acute and long-term care settings, the objectives of the comprehensive plans are to restrict utilization to its lowest-cost alternatives consistent with established standards for the quality of care. As in acute care, the lowest-cost, long-term care setting may be the most comfortable one for the patient as well as the least expensive. Moreover, incentives exist in the capitated, comprehensive health plans to provide quality care both to discourage enrollees from leaving the plans and, perhaps more importantly, to encourage nonmembers to enroll.

Continuing care retirement communities are prepaid, long-term care organizations that provide residential units, social services, and nursing home facilities for their residents. Individuals usually pay a capital fee upon enrollment and a monthly membership fee thereafter. As of the mid-1980s, more than 100,000 individuals had enrolled in approximately 600 CCRCs (Ruchlin 1988). Since the capital fee may vary from $10,000 to $100,000, the scrutiny of the CCRCs' financial integrity has been seen as a prime area for government regulation (Cohen 1980). Thus far, however, there have been no studies of the quality of care CCRCs deliver or the extent to which they can control long-term care costs.

Social/health maintenance organizations (integrated case-management systems) began providing services in 1983 under an HCFA demonstration project in four locations: Portland, Oregon; Brooklyn, New York; Minneapolis, Minnesota; and Long Beach, California. S/HMOs differ from CCRCs in that S/HMOs include an acute care component in addition to long-term care. S/HMOs provide Medicare-covered acute care services, but with no copayments or deductibles. In addition, there is no apartment-living component in S/HMOs as there is in CCRCs. In both CCRCs and S/HMOs, however, a single provider is responsible for all of the care under a prospective budget and is at risk for costs exceeding this budget. Monthly S/HMO premiums vary from $25 to $49.

Rivlin and Weiner (1988) have suggested that adequate enrollment has generally been a problem for S/HMOs since individuals would like to remain with their own physician. Newcomer, Harrington, and Friedlob (1990) in their examination of the HCFA demonstration project also found disappointing enrollments, perhaps due to competition from HMOs, suboptimal marketing, and the limited size of their geographic market area. Thus far, there have been no studies on the extent to which S/HMOs may or may not be able to contain costs.

Another form of comprehensive care, Life Care at Home, emphasizes noninstitutional, home-based care for the elderly. Care may include skilled nursing care, home delivered meals, respite care, and pharmacy and emergency services. Acute health care benefits might also be an option. The Life Care at Home model may be less expensive than the CCRC model since subscribers are encouraged to live in their own homes as long as possible, a feature which most elderly prefer (Tell, Cohen, and Wallack 1987).

Long-Term Care in the Future

The pressures for an increased number of long-term care services that an aging population will demand suggest that there will be a continuing response from the supply side either in an increase in the variety and number of different forms of long-term care or in higher prices for existing long-term care services. Total costs will increase in any event. The public policy challenge will be to finance the most efficient forms of long-term care without increasing the costs associated with the moral hazard of the care.

Currently, Medicaid, as the largest payer, reimburses primarily for nursing home care, which creates a reimbursement system sustaining many people in nursing homes who could be cared for at home in a less costly manner; moreover, many disabled adults at home need to be attended to in a nursing home setting but are not able to secure a room. Under Section 2176 of the Omnibus Budget Reconciliation Act of 1981, states, through waivers, may reimburse for home care and community-based care for those who would ordinarily need institutionalization (Meltzer 1988).

Integrated case-management plans have incentives to place individuals in the least costly setting. In addition, as Bishop (1988) points out, the integrated firms have an advantage over the individuals themselves in controlling the expensive costs in the nursing home. This is because the integrated firm has more bargaining power than a single individual as well as more information, based on a large number of patients, on the prices and qualities of the various homes. Alternatively, because of moral hazard, higher long-term care costs may result. If S/HMOs or other integrated plans were to compete, incentives for cream-skimming would arise as they do in acute care. Indeed, a large part of the argument for government intervention in this industry is private insurers' potential avoidance of high-risk individuals.

References

Bishop, C. E. (1988). "Competition in the Market for Nursing Home Care." In *Competition in the Health Care Sector: Ten Years Later*, ed W. Greenberg, 119–38. Durham, NC: Duke University Press.

Cohen, D. L. (1980). "Continuing Care Communities for the Elderly: Potential Pitfalls and Proposed Regulation," *University of Pennsylvania Law Review* 128: 882–936.

Feder, J., and Scanlon, W. (1980). "Regulating the Bed Supply in Nursing Homes," *Milbank Memorial Fund Quarterly* 58 (no. 1): 54–88.

Health Care Financing Administration, Office of National Cost Estimates (1990). "National Health Care Expenditures, 1988" *Health Care Financing Review* 11 (no. 4): 1–41.

Holahan, J. F. (1985). "State Rate-Setting and its Effects on the Cost of Nursing Home Care," *Journal of Health Politics, Policy and Law* 9: 647–67.

Holahan, J. F., and Cohen, J. W. (1987). *Medicaid: The Trade-off Between Cost Containment and Access to Care.* Washington, DC: The Urban Institute.

Kovar, M. G., Hendershot, G., and Mathis, E. (1989). "Older People in the United States Who Receive Help With Basic Activities of Daily Living," *American Journal of Public Health* 79: 778–79.

Medicine and Health Perspectives (1989). "Quality Data: How Good Is It?" *Medicine and Health Perspectives,* 1–4. Washington, DC: McGraw-Hill.

Meiners, M. R. (1989). *Public Attitudes on Long-Term Care.* Washington, DC: Health Insurance Association of America.

Meltzer, J. W. (1988). "Financing Long-Term Care: A Major Obstacle to Reform." In *The Economics and Ethics of Long-Term Care and Disability,* eds. S. Sullivan and M. E. Lewin, 56–72. Washington, DC: American Enterprise Institute.

Newcomer, R., Harrington, C., and Friedlob, A. (1990). "Social Health Maintenance Organizations: Assessing Their Initial Experience," *Health Services Research* 25: 425–54.

New York Times (1989). "Ford to Test Health Plan for Long-Term Care," (March 20).

———. (1987). "Week in Review," (February 15).

Nyman, J. A. (1989). "Excess Demand, Consumer Rationality, and the Quality of Care in Regulated Nursing Homes," *Health Services Research* 24: 105–27.

———. (1988). "The Effect of Competition on Nursing Home Expenditures under Prospective Reimbursement," *Health Services Research* 23: 555–74.

Rivlin, A. M., and Wiener, J. M. (1988). *Caring for the Disabled Elderly. Who Will Pay?* Washington, DC: Brookings Institution.

Ruchlin, H. S. (1988). "Continuing Care Retirement Communities: An Analysis of Financial Viability and Health Care Coverage," *The Gerontologist* 28: 156–62.

Tell, E. J., Cohen, M. A., and Wallack, S. S. (1987). "Life Care at Home: A New Model for Financing and Delivering Long-Term Care," *Inquiry* 24: 245–52.

Van Gelder, S., and Johnson, D. (1989). *Long-Term Care Insurance: Market Trends.* Washington, DC: Health Insurance Association of America.

Vogel, R. J. (1983). "The Industrial Organization of the Nursing Home Industry." In *Long-Term Care Perspectives from Research and Demonstrations,* eds. R. J. Vogel and H. C. Palmer, 579–624. Washington, DC: U.S. Department of Health and Human Services.

Weissert, W., and Scanlon, W. (1985). "Determinants of Nursing Home Discharge Status," *Medical Care* 23: 333–43.

10

Technology and Rationing

Economists have found it difficult to identify how much of the increase in health care costs may be due to technology. This is due, in part, to the interrelationship between insurance and technology: the introduction of expensive technology raises costs, which in time engenders increased insurance reimbursement, which may lead to newer technology. Other variables, such as changes in real income and population, may also add to health care costs, but these variables are highly correlated with new technology (Goddeeris 1984; Goddeeris and Weisbrod 1985). Researchers have suggested that as much as 50 percent of the increase in hospital costs stems from new technology (Evans 1983; Schwartz 1987; Hillman 1986). Not all new technology leads to rising health care costs, however. For example, the prices of soft contact lenses fell 50 percent between 1971 and 1982 (U.S. Congress, Office of Technology Assessment 1984, 29–30). Soft contact lenses, however, unlike most other health care technologies, are rarely paid for by third-party insurers.

In many other industries in the economy, real prices may fall over time as new technology leads to savings in labor costs and economies of scale in production. For example, when the video cassette recorder (VCR) was first sold to the public in 1978 its average unit price was $811. In 1990, its average unit price was $290 (Electronic Industries Association 1989). Firms in non–health care industries have incentives to use improved technology to reduce costs (and to increase quality), so as to become more competitive with other firms.

New technology may also stimulate increased utilization. For example, the number of cataract surgeries increased from 350,000 in 1978 to 1.4 million in 1987 as cataract surgery shifted largely from an inpatient to an outpatient procedure (Samuelson 1988, A–23). For Medicare beneficiaries, the number of cataract surgeries increased from 17.49 procedures per 1,000 Medicare beneficiaries in 1983 to 26.21 procedures per 1,000 in 1986, a 49.9 percent increase (Mitchell, Wedig, and Cromwell 1989). In part, this may have been due to the greater willingness of insuring organizations to reimburse on an outpatient rather than an inpatient basis, but it may also have been due to the reduction of risk involved in the surgery, the increased success rate, the reduced pain after surgery, and the reduced "time cost" of hospitalization.

In the same manner, Medicare's decision to pay for kidney dialysis enabled a greater number of individuals to be dialyzed at outpatient centers rather than at home. This reduced the financial and emotional burden on family members but greatly increased the number of people who would be able to undertake dialysis. The result has been increased real costs for this technology (Schwartz 1987).

Diffusion of Medical Technology

New technology is not immediately adopted by each firm in an industry. Firms have different capital requirements, purchasing cycles, production functions, and profit levels. Because of reimbursement trends, technology adoption may vary between outpatient and inpatient settings. Russell (1979, 158–59) found that, among hospitals, the more prestigious technologies were more likely to be adopted by the largest hospitals (in terms of number of beds) than by the smallest hospitals.

Hillman and Schwartz (1985) looked at the adoption and diffusion of computerized axial tomography (CT) and magnetic resonance imaging (MRI) devices. They found that in hospital settings, the CT, a diagnostic imaging device, had a much more rapid diffusion rate than the more costly MRI, also a diagnostic imaging device but with no radiation exposure and little patient discomfort. In nonhospital settings, the adoption rate was about the same. Apparently, the uncertainty about whether DRGs would continue to reimburse the capital costs of new equipment delayed a more widespread adoption of the MRI in hospitals. Moreover, more than four years after the introduction of the MRI, only 14 of 70 Blue Cross plans reimbursed MRI procedures (Steinberg, Sisk, and Locke 1985). Hillman and Schwartz (1985) also reported that most of the hospitals that did purchase MRI units were academic center hospitals, which may put greater emphasis on new technology. In addition, Steinberg, Sisk, and Locke (1985) suggested that the relatively slow diffusion of the MRI systems may stem from the belief that the incremental marginal benefits for magnetic resonance imagers are relatively less than for CT scanners. Moreover, perhaps due to the DRG reimbursement being limited to inpatient settings only, a proportionately greater number of MRIs than CT scanners have been installed in outpatient rather than inpatient areas (Steinberg, Sisk, and Locke 1985).

Sloan, Valvona, and Perrin (1986), in an analysis of five surgical procedures at 521 hospitals between 1971 and 1981, found evidence (although weak) that technology diffusion is more likely to occur in teaching hospitals than in nonteaching hospitals, a conclusion that supports Hillman and Schwartz's (1985) findings. According to Sloan, Valvona, and Perrin (1986) payment mechanisms, such as rate setting by states, have had little effect on the pattern of diffusion except for a small negative effect on the use of coronary bypass surgery.

What seems clear from these studies of diffusion is that not every hospital or health care entity adopts technology as soon as it is available. Those who might argue that the presence of third-party insurance automatically means that all hospitals and other health care entities run up costs indiscriminately are in error.

Cost Containment and Medical Technology

Since medical technology appears to account for a significant proportion of the increase in health care costs, public policy has attempted to exert control over the spread of technology. The two most common forms of control have been certificate-of-need laws and mandatory state rate-setting programs. DRGs, as we shall see, have attempted to control increases in technology in an indirect manner.

In Chapter 7 we saw that certificate-of-need laws had little effect on capital investment. Sloan, Valvona, and Perrin (1986) also found in their study of diffusion of surgical technology that certificate-of-need laws had no effect on cost containment and that mandatory state rate-setting programs had no effect on the diffusion of technology in four of the five surgical procedures they studied (coronary bypass surgery being the exception). On the other hand, Cromwell and Kanak (1982), in a sample of more than 2,500 hospitals, found that rate-setting programs had a "consistent, retarding effect" on the adoption of technology in New York and a "retarding effect" in other rate-setting states between 1969 and 1978. Capital equipment for intensive care units, open-heart surgery, physical therapy, and social work departments, as well electroencephalograms and radioisotopes were most affected by prospective reimbursement programs. In a later study that used a sample of more than 2,700 hospitals between 1970 and 1979 Cromwell (1987) found that state hospital rate-setting programs had little effect on capital formation. In New York and Massachusetts, however, rate setting appeared to reduce the rate of bed growth.

Capital technology and growth are pass-through costs under the federal DRG program. Although capital costs (defined as interest, depreciation, rent, and a return on equity for investor-owned hospitals) are only 7 percent of total hospital costs, capital will, of course, influence the magnitude of operating costs (Anderson and Ginsburg 1984). The fact that hospitals are in different stages of their technology-adoption cycle makes it difficult for the government to utilize a uniform target for the payment of new technologies for all hospitals covered under the DRG program. However, the marginal or operating costs incurred from new capital technology are covered under the DRG program. Moreover, although capital expenses are still paid on a cost basis, Medicare may reduce the payment for capital expenses by a specific percentage.

Kane and Manoukian (1989) point out that, even under the DRG system, cost-increasing technologies may be indirectly controlled. By placing cost-increasing technologies, such as implantable defibrillators, under DRGs that would not cover the costs of the new technology, adoption and diffusion may be retarded. Technologies with potential for cost reduction, such as extracorporeal shock-wave lithotripsy, would be placed under DRGs that would most probably fully cover their costs, thereby creating incentives for adoption.

Pharmaceuticals

Although pharmaceuticals are generally not considered part of the medical technology industry, they are often used in conjunction with medical technology and sometimes may substitute for medical technology. Drugs and pharmaceuticals make up less than 10 percent of U.S. expenditures for health care, with the value of 1988 shipments estimated at $41.3 billion, an increase of more than one-third over the 1985 figure of $31.3 billion. Of the 1988 amount, approximately $3.6 billion of pharmaceuticals was imported (U.S. Department of Commerce 1989, 16-1–16-3).

More than 750 firms were in the pharmaceutical industry as of 1988. Four firms controlled 23 percent of the industry, although that concentration figure would not, of course, be applicable to a particular drug (Pharmaceutical Manufacturers Association 1989). In 1987, the industry spent $5.4 billion on research and development and introduced 21 new drugs (U.S. Department of Commerce, 1989, 16–1). Despite these figures, some believe that technological development has been hindered by the 1962 amendments to the original Food, Drug, and Cosmetic Act of 1938, which had required that drugs be adequately tested for safety. The 1962 drug amendments required not only safety but also proof of efficacy. According to Peltzman (1973), the extra costs involved in meeting the tests of efficacy have hindered the research and development of new drugs.

Some pharmaceuticals have the potential to reduce health care costs. Vaccines for tetanus and poliomyelitis, for example, have been shown to be very cost effective (Weisbrod and Huston 1983). Likewise, prophylactic antibiotics have been shown to be cost effective (Kaiser 1986). In contrast, it is not clear that medications are cost effective in treating hypertension (Weinstein and Stason 1985).

Pharmaceuticals are not covered under the Medicare program. However, 47 of the 49 states that participate in Medicaid pay for prescription drugs and 44 percent of all prescription drug expenditures are covered by third-party payers (Office of National Cost Estimates 1990, 14).

Trends in Health Care Costs

Most studies have shown that, for any given point in time, health maintenance organizations have lower costs than the indemnity plans in the fee-for-service sector. However, two longitudinal studies (from 1961 to 1974 and from 1976 to 1981) showed that the rate of increase in HMO costs is about the same as the rate of increase in fee-for-service costs (Luft 1980; Newhouse, Schwartz, Williams, and Witsberger 1985). Since health maintenance organizations have lower costs than the fee-for-service sector, similar rates of increase imply slightly greater absolute increases in costs in the fee-for-service sector. Newhouse, Schwartz, Williams, and Witsberger (1985) suggest that this trend in health care costs may be due to the fee-for-service sector's greater use of technology, but they suggest also that HMOs are adopting most of the new technology. A later study by Newhouse (1988) also shows that much of the increase in health care costs is due to the adoption of new technology. Schwartz (1987) similarly finds that the adoption and diffusion of new technology is largely responsible for rising health care costs. In contrast, the aging of the population and the costs of malpractice insurance have had inconsequential effects.

There appear to be at least two reasons why the adoption of new technology continues to increase. First, as this chapter has suggested, there have not been effective regulatory controls of technology under prospective reimbursement methods. Second, there is demand for the implementation of medically efficacious practices and procedures without regard to their economic efficiency (Schwartz and Joskow 1978).

An example may show the difference between medically efficacious and economically efficient practices and procedures. Suppose that physicians were able to determine the potential benefits and costs of the utilization of new technologies. Assume that the benefits from using a new technology were $500 including, if it could be valued, the increased value of life from successful medical intervention. Assume the costs were $400 including, if they could be valued, the pecuniary costs of the procedure, the cost of pain, and the costs of waiting and inconvenience. Physicians, in this case, would perform the test or procedure for it would be medically efficacious. Economists, in this case, would agree with this course of action because benefits would exceed costs and the procedure would be economically efficient.

Suppose, however, that the benefits had a zero value and the costs of the procedure were $500. Ethical physicians would not perform the procedure since it would not be medically efficacious. Economists would agree with this medical decision since the procedure would also not be economically efficient. The conflict between medical efficacy and economic efficiency occurs when the costs of a procedure are $500 and the benefits are greater than zero but less than $500. Physicians would normally go ahead with the procedure since there are some positive benefits to be gained; the procedure would be considered medically efficacious. Economists, in contrast, would view the procedure as inefficient because costs exceed benefits.

According to Schwartz and Joskow (1978), there are a large number of procedures in which costs exceed benefits yet the benefits are greater than zero. Thus, it becomes difficult for third-party payers to contain costs. The individual benefits from such procedures, but from society's standpoint they are economically inefficient.

Because of the conflict between medical efficacy and economic efficiency, phrases such as unnecessary surgery and unnecessary hospitalization are vague and ambiguous. To the economist, surgery or hospitalization that does not pass a cost-benefit test will be considered unnecessary. To the physician and insured patient (both of whom are unconcerned about pecuniary cost), unnecessary surgery is when benefits are virtually zero.

The conflict between medical efficacy and economic efficiency can be seen most vividly in the decision in *Wickline v. California* 192 Cal. App. 3d 1630, 236 Cal. Rptr. 810 (1986). In that case, a patient, Lois Wickline, was admitted to a hospital in California for surgery for circulatory and vascular ailments. After she developed problems from the surgery, her physician requested Medicaid approval for an additional eight days. Medi-Cal, the California state Medicaid agency, only approved an additional stay of four days. After Wickline's discharge, she developed increased circulatory problems that culminated with the surgical removal of her leg. Wickline sued the Medi-Cal authorities for refusing to pay for the length of stay recommended by her doctor.

The California Second District Court of Appeals ruled that, in fact, the Medi-Cal officials had a legitimate reason to believe that the additional four days were unnecessary and, in this particular case, were exonerated from any responsibility. The most important part of the decision, however, was that third-party payers could be held responsible in the future for curtailing utilization in which there were some benefits to be gained. That is, as long as there were benefits to be gained for the individual, third parties could not contain utilization even though society might have valued those benefits at less than their costs. If procedures in which costs exceed benefits make up an increasing portion of health care expenditures, public policy may have to consider alternatives to competition and regulation, such as explicit rationing, to contain rising health care costs.

Definition of Rationing

Because of unlimited demand for limited resources, goods, and services, rationing takes place in every sector of the economy, including health care. The price system is the usual method of rationing goods and services. In competitive industries, price will equal the marginal cost of providing goods and services. The price system has the advantage of being completely impersonal and requiring no government intervention. For example, the price of a VCR at a particular store may be $300. Individuals may purchase a VCR at this price regardless of their race, sex, or age; the time they spent waiting in line; or their degree of influence or bargaining power with the store owner. Only those without $300 will be left out of the market. The same concept applies to most other goods and services. Society does not appear to be too concerned if some individuals cannot afford a VCR. For services like health care, on the other hand, society may be concerned if individuals do not receive at least some basic level of services.

Nonprice Rationing in Other Industries

Although the price system is the most efficient way of allocating goods and services, it is not always used in other industries. For example, although Super Bowl tickets have a face value price of perhaps $100, the final purchaser may pay more than five times that amount. In addition, a buyer may need friends and contacts to be able to obtain the tickets even at that higher price. Super Bowl tickets may, therefore, be allocated on a price basis (but at a much higher price than the price of a ticket) as well as by the influence of an individual buyer.

Rent control has been in force for more than one-half of the apartments in New York City since 1943. Apparently, rents are held below the equilibrium level; long waiting lists are established for the rent-controlled apartments. Thus, the rationing of apartments in New York is based on the rent that is charged and on the inclination of individuals to endure a substantial delay before obtaining an apartment.

Many goods and services may be rationed on a geographic basis in addition to a price basis. It is more costly, for example, in terms of time (opportunity cost) and transportation costs for an individual in, say, North Carolina to see a Broadway show than for someone who lives in New York. Rationing of incoming freshman slots at universities may be based on high school academic performance in addition to ability to pay tuition. Rationing of the "best tables" of a restaurant may be based on the repeat business and stature of customers in addition to the size of the tip to the maître d'.

Nonprice Rationing in Health Care

Nonprice rationing is not uncommon in the health care sector. Not everyone in the United States receives "presidential medicine." As Fuchs (1984) points out, health care may be rationed on a geographic basis because physicians are much more scarce (and the traveling time to see a physician is therefore greater) in Montana, for example, than in New York. The care in quality hospitals may also be rationed by nonprice mechanisms. Although hospitals are generally covered by insurance, not everyone has serious surgery at university hospitals that many perceive to be of superior quality or at "brand name" hospitals such as the Cleveland Clinic or the Mayo Clinic. Individuals who use these hospitals may be more careful shoppers of hospital care than others. There may also be nonprice rationing of intensive care units at many inner-city hospitals based on the condition of the patient. The reasons for rationing here may lie in the shortage of nurses, the aging of the population, the increase in violence, and the spread of AIDS (*Wall Street Journal* 1989, 1).

Within a specific disease, there has been explicit rationing in the United States. Kidney disease, for example, may be treated by traditional dialysis, continuous ambulatory peritoneal dialysis, or transplantation depending in large part on the physical condition of the patient. According to Held (1988), among those recommended for kidney transplantation there appears to be explicit rationing based on race, sex, age, health condition, and income. Patients who are white, male, young, nondiabetic, and high income have a greater likelihood of receiving a kidney transplant than other patients. Held speculates that perhaps blacks prefer dialysis over transplantation since, in fact, blacks do better than whites on regular dialysis. The willingness of relatives to donate kidneys may also be greater among whites than among blacks. In addition, although Medicare pays for the entire cost of transplantation, Medicare did not pay for the outpatient drugs during the time frame of the Held study (1980 to 1985) and still does not pay for transportation to and from the transplantation hospital. This, of course, means that low-income people are less likely to opt for transplants.

The rationing of a limited number of suitable kidneys may also reflect a bias of white male physicians who identify with white patients or who believe that black patients may be at greater risk in kidney transplants because of their more common ailments of hypertension and diabetes. The University of Pittsburgh has been less haphazard in allocating the shortage of cadaver kidneys in its hospital. The hospital has assigned points based on waiting time, antigen matching, antibody analysis, medical urgency, and logistical practicality. Each potential patient receives points based on these criteria (Starzl et al. 1987).

In fiscal year 1988, more than 900 individuals awaited a heart transplant in the United States. Most individuals who received transplants were white, male, and more than 45 years old. Eighty-four percent of all recipients were white (U.S. General Accounting Office 1989). It is not clear why this is so. Perhaps white patients, who in general have higher incomes than nonwhites and are more apt to be insured, more easily meet the hospital's financial criteria. Perhaps also because whites live longer than nonwhites, they are more apt to develop the heart disease that eventually dictates heart transplantation.

According to the U.S. General Accounting Office (1989), hospitals used both medical and financial criteria in selecting transplant patients. The survey of 18 hospitals found that individuals who had end-stage heart disease and who could not benefit from any other medical or surgical procedures would be the first to be selected. In regard to financial criteria, 3 of the 18 hospitals reported that transplant surgery could not begin unless payment was first assured. Fourteen hospitals said that some patients would be accepted without payment. One hospital did not provide its views on financial criteria.

The state of Oregon is the first public entity in the United States to attempt explicit rationing of procedures for its Medicaid patients. To extend basic Medicaid coverage to 1,500 additional individuals, the state has eliminated coverage of bone marrow, heart, liver, and pancreas transplantations. These transplants were projected to cost approximately $2.2 million for 34 patients between 1987 and 1989 (Welch and Larson 1988; *Washington Post* 1988, A-1, A-6). Apparently concerned with only the most expensive transplant procedures, Oregon would still cover the less expensive procedures such as cornea and kidney transplants under the state Medicaid provisions. Individuals, in addition, can still use commercial insurance to pay for coverage, can solicit donations, or can move to another state in order to receive a rationed transplant.

An even more ambitious rationing scheme by the state of Oregon is its ranking of 1,600 medical procedures by priority of treatment. In this ranking system, the costs of the procedure would be weighed against the benefits. The benefits would be calculated as the number of years that a patient would benefit, multiplied by a "quality of well-being" index. This index, agreed upon by a number of health experts, is based on such subjective criteria as the time before the ailment could recur and the patient's health after treatment (*New York Times* 1990, p. 1).

Another approach to nonprice rationing would be rationing based on age. Researchers have examined health care expenditures for the aged population relative to expenditures for the nonaged population. Fisher (1980) found that persons who are older than 65 incur 29 percent of all health care expenditures, but represent only 11 percent of the population. Moreover, Fisher found that in 1978 the average annual medical expenses for those aged 65 and over were $2,026, compared to $764 for individuals aged 19 to 64 and $286 for individuals under age 19. In a later, closely related study, Berk, Monheit, Hagan et al. (1988) found that 1 percent of the population accounted for 29 percent of health care expenditures, and that more than 43 percent of this group was over the age of 65. Yet rationing by age is also subjective. For example, at what age does rationing begin? Should all procedures be rationed? Should health status be taken into account in the rationing process?

In addition to nonprice rationing, there is still rationing by price in the health care system. As we saw in Chapter 4, patients are sensitive to copayments and deductibles, especially for ambulatory care. In Chapter 11, we will explore rationing in Canada, Great Britain, and the Netherlands to examine the extent to which rationing as well as competition and regulation may be needed in the United States in the future.

References

Anderson, G., and Ginsburg, P. B. (1984). "Medicare Payment and Hospital Capital: Future Policy Options," *Health Affairs* 3: 35–48.

Berk, M. L., Monheit, A. C., Hagan, M. M., et al. (1988). "How the U.S. Spends Its Health Care Dollar: 1929–80," *Health Affairs* 7: 46–60.

Cromwell, J. (1987). "Impact of State Hospital Rate Setting on Capital Formation," *Health Care Financing Review* 8 (no. 3): 69–82.

Cromwell, J., and Kanak, J. R. (1982). "The Effects of Prospective Reimbursement Programs on Hospital Adoption and Service Sharing," *Health Care Financing Review* 4 (no. 2): 67–88.

Electronic Industries Association (1989). *Consumer Electronics Annual Review.* Washington, DC: Electronic Industries Association.

Evans, R. W. (1983). "Health Care Technology and the Inevitability of Resource Allocation and Rationing Decisions," *Journal of the American Medical Association* 249: 2047–57.

Fisher, C. R. (1980). "Differences by Age Groups in Health Care Spending," *Health Care Financing Review* 1 (no. 4): 65–90.

Fuchs, V. R. (1984). "The 'Rationing' of Medical Care," *The New England Journal of Medicine* 311 (no. 24): 1572–73.

Goddeeris, J. H. (1984). "Medical Insurance, Technological Change, and Welfare," *Economic Inquiry* 22: 56–67.

Goddeeris, J. H., and Weisbrod, B. (1985). "What We Don't Know About Why Health Expenditures Have Soared: Interaction of Insurance and Technology," *Mount Sinai Journal of Medicine* 52: 685–91.

Held, P. J. (1988). "Access to Kidney Transplantation," *Archives of Internal Medicine* 148: 2594–600.

Hillman, A. L., and Schwartz, J. S. (1985). "The Adoption and Diffusion of CT and MRI in the United States, A Comparative Analysis," *Medical Care* 23 (no. 11): 1283–94.

Hillman, B. J. (1986). "Government Health Policy and the Diffusion of New Medical Devices," *Health Services Research* 21 (no. 5): 681–711.

Kaiser, A. (1986). "Antimicrobial Prophylaxis in Surgery," *The New England Journal of Medicine* 315: 1129–38.

Kane, N. M., and Manoukian, P. D. (1989). "The Effect of the Medicare Prospective Payment System on the Adoption of New Technology," *The New England Journal of Medicine* 321 (no. 20): 1378–83.

Luft, H. S. (1980). "Trends in Medical Care Costs," *Medical Care* 18: 1–16.

Mitchell, J. B., Wedig, G., and Cromwell, J. (1989). "The Medicare Physician Fee Freeze: What Really Happened?" *Health Affairs* 8: 21–33.

National Pharmaceutical Council (1986). *Pharmaceutical Benefits Under State Medical Assistance Programs.* Reston, VA: National Pharmaceutical Council.

New York Times (1990). "Oregon Lists Illnesses by Priority to See Who Gets Medicaid Care," (May 3): 1.

Newhouse, J. P. (1988). "Has the Erosion of the Medical Marketplace Ended?" In *Competition in the Health Care Sector: Ten Years Later*, ed. W. Greenberg, 41–56. Durham, NC: Duke University Press.

Newhouse, J. P., Schwartz, W. B., Williams, A. P., and Witsberger, C. (1985). "Are Fee-for-Service Costs Increasing Faster than HMO Costs?" *Medical Care* 23: 960–66.

Office of National Cost Estimates (1990). "National Health Expenditures, 1988," *Health Care Financing Review* 11: 1–41.

Peltzman, S. (1973). "An Evaluation of Consumer Protection Legislation: The 1962 Drug Amendments," *Journal of Political Economy* 81 (no. 5): 1049–91.

Pharmaceutical Manufacturers Association (1989). *PMA Statistical Fact Book.* Washington, DC: Pharmaceutical Manufacturers Association.

Russell, L. B. (1979). *Technology in Hospitals: Medical Advances and Their Diffusion.* Washington, DC: Brookings Institution.

Samuelson, R. J. (1988). "Why Medical Costs Keep Soaring," *Washington Post* (November 30): A-23.

Schwartz, W. B. (1987). "The Inevitable Failure of Cost Containment Strategies," *Journal of American Medical Association* 257 (no. 2): 220–24.

Schwartz, W. B., and Joskow, P. L. (1978). "Medical Efficacy versus Economic Efficiency," *The New England Journal of Medicine* 299: 1452–64.

Sloan, F. A., Valvona, J., and Perrin, J. M. (1986). "Diffusion of Surgical Technology: An Exploratory Study," *Journal of Health Economics* 5: 31–61.

Starzl, T. E. et al. (1987). "A Multifactorial System for Equitable Selection of Cadaver Kidney Recipients," *Journal of the American Medical Association* 257: 3073–75.

Steinberg, E. P., Sisk, J. E., and Locke, K. E. (1985). "X-Ray CT and Magnetic Resonance Imagers," *The New England Jouranl of Medicine* 313 (no. 14): 859–64.

U.S. Congress, Office of Technology Assessment (1984). *Federal Policies and the Medical Device Industry*, OTA-H-230. Washington, DC: U.S. Government Printing Office.

U.S. Department of Commerce (1989). *U.S. Industrial Outlook, 1989—Medical Instruments.* Washington, DC: U.S. Government Printing Office.

U.S. General Accounting Office (1989). *Heart Transplants, Concerns About Cost, Access, and Availability of Donor Organs.* Washington, DC: U.S. Government Printing Office.

Wall Street Journal (1989). "Intensive-Care Units Are Rejecting Patients Because of Crowding," (May 23): 1.

Washington Post (1988). "Rising Cost of Medical Treatment Forces Oregon to 'Play God,' " (February 5): A-1.

Weinstein, M. C., and Stason, W. B. (1985). "Cost-effectiveness of Interventions to Prevent or Treat Coronary Heart Disease," *Annual Review of Public Health* 6: 41–63.

Weisbrod, B. A., and Huston, J. (1983). *Benefits and Costs of Human Vaccines in Developed Countries: An Evaluative Survey,* Report #2. Washington, DC: Pharmaceutical Manufacturers Association.

Welch, H. G., and Larson, E. B. (1988). "The Oregon Decision to Curtail Funding for Organ Transplantation," *The New England Journal of Medicine* 319 (no. 3): 171–73.

11

Insights from Canada, Great Britain, and the Netherlands

Economic theory suggests that as an industry becomes more competitive, firms become more efficient. They also experience competitive rates of return rather than realize monopoly profits. We have seen, however, that in the health care sector the presence of insurance leads to expenditures that may be efficient from the individual's point of view but inefficient from society's perspective because the increase in expenditures may exceed the marginal benefits to society. Moreover, competition in the health care industry does not by itself guarantee an equitable distribution of services or necessarily lead to a reduction in rising costs. If there are upward shifts in demand, there will be increases in prices and expenditures just as there would be in other industries. An increase in the input costs of providing health care services will also exert upward pressure on prices.

In this chapter I will describe how three countries—Canada, Great Britain, and the Netherlands—have attempted to achieve efficiency, equity, and cost containment in health care services. Each country has selected a different mix of competition, regulation, and rationing to achieve these goals. Examination of the three approaches may yield insights into how competition, regulation, and rationing may be used to vary the mixture of efficiency, equity, and cost containment in U.S. health care services.

The Canadian Health Care System

In the Canadian health care system, there is less competition and much more regulation than is the case in the United States. In Canada, each of the ten provinces finances health care for every individual in the province. Private-sector insurance is prohibited for hospital and physician services that are covered by the province. Providers are also prohibited from taking private-pay patients if they treat patients under government financing. The driving force behind the Canadian system is universal, equal, and complete first-dollar coverage for hospital and physician services, including inpatient prescription drugs and outpatient tests and procedures. Mental health care is also completely covered (Iglehart 1990, 563). Consequently, unlike nearly every other Western country, Canada has no private-sector loophole for affluent persons. In addition, the lack of competition among insurers precludes competition to avoid high-risk individuals or to set higher premiums for those with higher-cost illnesses.

Outpatient drugs, dental services, optometry, physiotherapy, and cosmetic surgery, perhaps considered discretionary purchases, are not covered by the provincial plans (Iglehart 1990, 562). In addition, well-off Canadians can and do go outside the country (mostly to the United States) for health care services.

Insurance is financed through the tax system. Physicians practice medicine on a private, fee-for-service basis, receiving fees that have been negotiated with each province. Since 1976 some provinces have also negotiated aggregate billing targets with physicians to attempt to cut down on tests and procedures. Fees are subsequently reduced if target ceilings are exceeded. Balance billing (billing patients for fees above the allowed amount) is prohibited to ensure equal access to physicians regardless of one's income.

Hospitals, which are generally nonprofit, negotiate the size of their operating budget with each province. New capital facilities and renovations must be approved by the province for the hospital to receive funding for them. Even if a hospital were to receive funding for capital equipment from philanthropic contributions, the province might not supply the operating funds. In addition, health care costs are controlled by limiting hospital expansion and by limiting high-technology equipment to certain regions or to teaching hospitals. Further, to reduce costs, diagnostic services are centralized in hospitals or approved private laboratories rather than in physicians' offices (Evans 1983; Evans et al. 1989; Iglehart 1990).

In the Canadian system, individuals have free choice of physician and hospital. Long waiting times have, however, been reported for open-heart and other major surgeries. There is no price or quality competition among hospitals or physicians, no opportunities for providers to gain competitive advantage as members of preferred provider organizations or managed-care plans. Physicians perceived to be of higher quality cannot charge their patients more than other physicians; physicians who wish to charge less than the negotiated rate are prohibited from doing so. Canada spent 8.6 percent of its gross national product on health care in 1987, a smaller proportion than the United States but a greater amount than the 7.4 percent Canada spent when the health care system was introduced in 1971 (Evans et al. 1989, 571, 572). Although there is universal access, with no price barriers to needed hospital and physician services, there is no competition among insuring organizations to contain costs. In short, there is no market in which insuring organizations can negotiate the prices of hospital and physician services and in which individuals can choose plans based on quality and price.

The British Health Care System

The British health care system differs in many respects from the U.S. and Canadian health care systems. In Great Britain, most physicians do not practice private, fee-for-service medicine but receive a salary from the British government. The salary of general practitioners is based customarily on the number of patients for whom they have responsibility, while specialists receive a salary regardless of the number of patients they have.

Hospitals receive a budget from the government for construction and capital equipment as well as for current operating expenses. In 1988, British health care expenditures were only 6.2 percent of the gross national product, a small increase from the 5.5 percent of the gross national product in 1975 and the 5.8 percent of the gross national product in 1980 (Schieber and Pouillier 1989).

Approximately 12 percent of total medical expenditures are accounted for by individuals who use private physicians and facilities to avoid queues for medical procedures (Aaron and Schwartz 1984, 22). According to Aaron and Schwartz (1984, 16), waiting times for British hospitals are three months or more for as many as one-third of patients.

The British spend one-half the amount per capita on hospital care that the United States spends. In Great Britain, about one-half as many x-rays are taken; coronary artery bypass surgery is performed at a rate of only 10 percent compared to that of the United States; and there are one-fifth to one-tenth the number of intensive care beds. Like the

Canadian system, the British system places a high regard on equity; each citizen is automatically insured by the government, with little or no copayment. Limitations are placed on the size of hospital medical staffs, on the amount of technical equipment, on new experimental procedures, and on the construction of new hospitals.

To contain costs, the British ration health care on an explicit basis. Criteria may seem somewhat arbitrary. For example, at one time physicians did not recommend kidney dialysis for those over the age of 55 because dialysis was believed to be too costly. Since the development of continuous ambulatory peritoneal dialysis, a lower-cost procedure, physicians have begun to recommend dialysis for those over age 55. Still, kidney dialysis is done only one-third as often in Great Britain as in the United States. Total parenteral nutrition is performed at only one-fourth the U.S. rate. Some rationing may not be based on medical evidence alone. For example, physicians may be reluctant to perform coronary bypass surgery on those who are suffering from angina pectoris or chest pain because this disease is not visible to the general public. In contrast, victims of hemophilia, a more-visible disease, are treated more quickly. "Dread" diseases, such as cancer, are also treated with little rationing.

Great Britain spends a greater proportion of its health care resources on children than the United States. Health expenditures per child in England are 119 percent of expenditures for prime-age adults, whereas expenditures for children in the United States are only 37 percent as much as for prime-age adults. If one takes into consideration the potential of future productivity, the stress on health care for the younger population may be economically sound (Aaron and Schwartz 1984; Aaron and Schwartz 1990).

The British health care system relies on government control of hospital expenditures and physician salaries to contain health care costs. Currently, however, 9 percent of the population has opted for private health insurance, and 17 percent of elective surgery is performed in the private sector (Lister 1989, 878). In an effort to inject some competition into the system, the government published a white paper in 1989 calling for hospitals with more than 250 beds to govern themselves and bid competitively to provide services to local health authorities. Physician group practices with more than 11,000 patients were invited to negotiate with hospitals to provide hospital care for their patients (Lister 1989, 877, 878). It remains to be seen whether this proposed increase in competiton will lead to lower costs or to greater inequities in the health care system.

The Dutch Health Care System

It is instructive to examine both the current Dutch health care system and the proposed changes in health care financing and distribution expected to take place in the Netherlands by the mid-1990s. The current system includes a compulsory sickness-fund component with a standard benefit package of physician, hospital, and some dental services for employees and their dependents earning less than $25,000 a year (including those who are unemployed), in which 62 percent of the country is enrolled; a noncompulsory, commercial-insurance component with a flexible benefit package for self-employed individuals and higher-income groups, in which 32 percent of the population is enrolled; and insurance for persons in public service (a sickness fund or commercial carrier may be selected), in which 6 percent of the population is enrolled (Netherlands Ministry of Welfare, Health, and Cultural Affairs 1988; van de Ven 1990). Currently, there are 30 sickness funds and 70 health insurance firms. In general, one-half of the premium of the sickness funds and the commercial health insurers is paid by the employer, and one-half paid by the employee. Sickness fund revenues are collected in a general fund, while premiums from the commercial health insurers are paid directly to the insurers themselves. In addition, the national health care program for all Dutch citizens, the compulsory Exceptional Medical Expenses (Compensation) Act, covers nursing home care, special institutional care for disabled individuals, and prolonged hospital stays. It is financed by income-related premiums paid by employees.

Fewer than 1 percent of the Dutch people do not have health insurance. Individuals who are eligible for insurance in a sickness fund are automatically enrolled. Individuals are allowed to continue with their insurance (commercial coverage or sickness fund) after leaving their employer group. Insurers cannot cancel an insurance contract if individuals incur large medical bills. Individuals who begin their working life in a self-employed job or who are making more than $25,000 a year and become seriously ill can continue with their original commercial insurance coverage. Individuals with higher medical expenses may, however, pay higher premiums for insurance, although there is a maximum premium that insurers can charge.

The Dutch health care system is highly regulated. This regulation has generated a number of inefficiencies, yet has still not solved the problem of an inequitable distribution of health services. Regulation has created barriers to competition from new potential entrants, existing providers, and alternative delivery systems. Regulation has also eliminated price competition among providers, and has eliminated choice of sickness funds by consumers.

The Dutch government regulates the supply of physicians. Family physicians can be prohibited from opening new practices when it is believed that an area already has an ample supply. The number of medical specialists is also limited to a preexisting "norm." The number and size of hospitals is regulated by the government. Hospitals are not permitted to increase the number of their beds or to invest in new technology without approval. In addition, the government approves the capacity of nursing homes as well as where they can be located. Limited provider plans, such as HMOs or PPOs are not allowed in the Netherlands. Each sickness fund and private insurer must contract with each provider in its geographic area.

Physician fees are uniform and are based on a national fee schedule that stems from negotiations between physicians and the sickness fund and commercial insurers. General practitioners receive a capitated fee from the sickness funds, but otherwise are paid on a fee-for-service basis. Medical specialists are always paid on a fee-for-service basis. The uniform fees paid to physicians eliminate price competition. Moreover, most patients are nearly fully insured and care little about price, although deductibles have become more common under private insurance. Hospitals also receive uniform payment based on their output, such as the number of admissions and negotiations between hospitals and the sickness funds and commercial insurers.

The sickness funds are each assigned a population from a particular region and are legally not allowed to compete against one another. Each sickness fund has no incentive to be efficient. They are reimbursed by the capital general fund according to the health expenditures of their members. If sickness funds are able to reduce costs through efficiency, reimbursement is reduced in the subsequent year.

Although one may have a choice among health insurers, they generally have not competed on a cost-containment basis. The uniform fees of physicians, the prohibition of limited provider plans, the potential boycott (due to the absence of antitrust legislation against providers) by providers against insurers if cost-containment activities were put into place, have all inhibited cost containment. Insurers, however, have competed by attracting low-risk individuals by introducing age-related premiums and inserting preexisting clauses in their contracts. Healthy individuals who are eligible for private health insurance may pay lower premiums than less affluent individuals in the sickness funds (Kirkman-Liff and van de Ven 1989; Lapre 1988; Netherlands Ministry of Welfare, Health, and Cultural Affairs 1988; van de Ven 1987; and van de Ven 1990).

Movement for change in the Dutch health care system

There appear to be a number of reasons why the Dutch government proposed an overhaul of their health care system. First, health care costs have shown a sharp upward trend. Health care costs represented 8.5 percent of the gross national product in 1990, up from 6.0 percent of the gross national product in 1970 and 3.3 percent in 1953. Second, the increased cream-skimming among private insurers created unacceptable inequities among the population. Third, the lack of incentives for cost containment by the sickness funds and the prohibitions against limited provider plans made it difficult to contain costs. Fourth, the regulation of the supply of physicians and hospitals became unworkable insofar as the optimal number of providers was difficult to calculate. Moreover, the providers themselves found regulation to be onerous and they became more amenable to a competitive alternative (Netherlands Ministry of Welfare, Health, and Cultural Affairs 1988; Kirkman-Liff and van de Ven 1989; van de Ven 1991).

In the new health care system proposed by the Dutch government, which is to be implemented by 1995, there is greater stress on equity, a much larger dose of allocative efficiency, and an increased emphasis on competition among insuring organizations (to be called "care insurers"). The new system is based on the consumer-choice health plan first proposed by Enthoven (1978) in *The New England Journal of Medicine.* Each individual or family will select a health plan from competing care insurers—HMOs, PPOs, or any form of indemnity plan—during an open-enrollment period every two years. Distinctions in purchasing a health plan between those who were employed with a firm, self-employed, or unemployed will be eliminated. However, employers can pay up to one-half of the health care premium for an employee if they still desire. The government will require care insurers to offer a substantially similar benefit package to all Dutch citizens to prevent skimpy benefit packages from being used as a device to attract only the healthiest persons. The benefit package will cover nearly all acute care, long-term care, and health care-related social welfare expenses. Individuals will also be free to purchase a supplemental plan that would pay for discretionary cosmetic surgery, abortions, and hospital amenities, such as private rooms, from among competing insurers.

Individuals must pay into a central fund a premium based on their income, and may pay to the plan of their choice an optional premium equal to approximately 10 percent of the average per capita costs of the covered benefits. This additional premium is independent of one's income and can vary by care insurer, creating incentives for care insurers to be efficient in order to reduce their premiums. The additional premium cannot be varied according to an individual's health.

In the new health care system, there will be universal health care coverage. Individuals with low incomes or who are unemployed would pay only a modest premium into the central fund, although insurance would be compulsory to avoid the free-rider problem of receiving coverage without payment. Plans would be reimbursed by the central fund equal to the number of their enrollees adjusted by their case mix. In addition, a budget cap would be placed on each care insurer equal to the degree of cost containment that the population desired. The central fund reimbursement, therefore, would accomplish two goals. First, plans would have less incentive to avoid high-risk individuals since capitation payment would be based, in part, on case mix. Second, plans would have incentives to contain costs to keep costs below the capitated rate. Moreover, plans that could deliver services more efficiently and with higher quality would enroll a larger number of people.

Competing care insurers would be expected to enter into contracts with hospitals and physicians for efficiency-improving measures such as preadmission review and other forms of utilization management. Unlike the current system, the proposed system would allow care insurers to contract selectively with efficient providers. Care insurers would not be allowed to deny coverage during the open-enrollment period, and insurers enrolling a disproportionate number of high-risk individuals would be compensated by the central fund dependent on their case mix. This case-mix adjustment would be based on such variables as the age, sex, and health status of a plan's enrollees. If it were calculated correctly, there would be little incentive for care insurers to avoid high-risk individuals. A prediction of utilization of health services based on prior utilization, functional health status (the ability to perform activities of daily living or the degree of one's infirmity), prior medical expenditure, disability, diagnostic information, and indicators of chronic medical conditions appear to be the most important factors in calculating the case-mix adjustment (van de Ven and van Vliet 1990). Thus far, researchers have been able to explain approximately two-thirds of the maximum explainable variance of about 15 percent in individual health expenditures with case-mix measures. Approximately

85 percent of the variance in individual health care expenditures is simply unexplained and unpredictable (Newhouse, Manning, Keller, and Sloss 1989; van de Ven and van Vliet 1990). Case-mix measures, however, may not need to be perfect because care insurers will also not be able to forecast the case mix of their population and their future expenses with precision. Additional research on case-mix measurement is, however, clearly needed. Cost containment would be achieved by competition among insuring organizations, by the budget cap placed on each insurer, and by potential governmental limits on the use of the most expensive technology.

Under the proposed system, the Dutch government would act like the "sponsor" envisioned by Enthoven (1988). It would ensure that the plans were financially viable, help individuals interpret the plans' provisions, determine the amount that the government and individuals would contribute, set the percentage sliding scale of premiums that individuals would pay, help individuals evaluate the quality of providers within each of the plans, and specify the basic benefit package of the health plans.

There is also an important information and antitrust component envisioned in the proposed Dutch health care system. Care insurers would be expected to advertise quality of providers, convenience of location, or other amenities associated with the plan. Some care insurers may inform prospective purchasers of their various cost-containment provisions. In addition, a number of consulting firms may begin to provide advice on the relative benefits of the care insurers. There may also be a governmental role to evaluate care insurers and for consumer protection to ensure that the insurers do not provide false and misleading advertising. The government would have an extensive antitrust role, especially in regard to anticompetitive hospital mergers and potential physician boycotts of cost-containment activities. The government would also have to monitor signs of potential collusion among care insurers.

There appear to be a number of advantages to the proposed Dutch health care system. It preserves incentives for care insurers to compete on innovative cost-containment measures. Plans that are more successful in controlling costs can realize greater revenues as well as increased market shares. Plans may also compete on quality of providers, quality of service, convenience, or any other basis. At the same time, the Dutch system attempts to eliminate competition among insuring organizations in avoiding high-risk individuals. There is a significant equity component in the proposed Dutch system since individuals pay premiums based, in large part, on income. Individuals cannot be refused health care insurance, and all individuals must purchase the standardized benefit package.

It is also important to understand a number of the other advantages of the proposed Dutch system. First, there are no Medicare or Medicaid components. There are no DRG price controls or physician fee schedules that create incentives to shift costs to other areas of the health care sector. Within the budget cap, there are incentives to use resources in their most efficient setting. Depending on how high or low it is set, the budget cap will force the health plans to eliminate services for which there are some marginal benefits but for which the costs to society substantially exceed the benefits. This will mean that every care insurer will have to ration or limit care within the organization. With a cap that covers both acute and long-term care expenditures, the organization, itself, will decide how best to allocate resources to maximize its income or number of enrollees or to achieve other goals it may have. Setting a cap on expenditures, however, could potentially choke off new technological advances that could achieve increased benefit the more often they are used. Another alternative is to couple a high cap with a change in the liability rules (see Chapter 10), such that medical procedures can be denied by the care insurer even if there are some marginal benefits from the procedure.

The proposed Dutch health care system may help improve productivity of the work force. In the United States, for example, seriously ill workers or families of seriously ill workers may be concerned about leaving a job for another more productive position for fear of losing health insurance. New employers may require medical examinations before health insurance enrollment can be allowed. Workers who wish to begin their own businesses will also have a difficult time securing coverage as individuals. Other workers may be reluctant to leave jobs to earn a higher educational degree. This lack of mobility represents a real loss of productivity and output for the worker and for the United States as a whole. A survey of 1,005 adults in December 1990 by International Communications Research of Media, Pennsylvania, found that 15 percent of those surveyed or family members of those surveyed had changed jobs or remained in their current jobs because of health insurance benefits (International Communications Research 1990).

Although individuals are concerned about retaining health insurance, there are approximately 27 million individuals employed in high-turnover industries—industries in which the average time spent on the job is 5 to 11 months. Examples of high-turnover industries include real estate, automotive repairs, eating and drinking places, and building construction. Employees in high-turnover industries may periodically face new employers and insuring organizations who will not cover preexisiting conditions. Moreover, employers incur high transactions costs (relative to the length of time of employment) in providing a health insurance plan, counseling the employee if a choice of plans is offered, and enrolling the individual (Schorr 1990). These transactions costs will make it increasingly unlikely that those industries will continue to offer health insurance.

In addition, the proposed Dutch system would eliminate financial inequities for those who currently have employer-based health insurance. In the United States, individuals employed with one firm may pay higher premiums for the same benefits package than individuals employed in another firm simply because of differences in the case mix of employees (Swartz 1990).

Summary and Conclusions

Canada, Great Britain, the Netherlands, and the United States emphasize differently, and with varying degrees of success, competition, regulation, and rationing in health care. Economics can be an important guide in explaining how these health care systems work and how they can be improved. Increased competition can play a significant role in achieving a more efficient allocation of resources. Competition, however, will not stem the long-running trend of rising health care expenditures, nor will it provide for a more equitable distribution of health care services.

Moreover, there are still impediments to a competitive health care system in the United States, such as the relatively primitive development of information on the quality and cost of providers. There have also been a number of anticompetitive actions in health care, including collective boycotts by providers of third-party payer cost-containment efforts, mergers between hospitals in highly concentrated markets, and restrictions placed by physicians on other health professionals. In addition, the pervasiveness of insurance in this industry leads to the use of services for which societal costs exceed societal benefits. There have also been regulations, such as certificate of need, that have been cost-increasing and economically inefficient. Other regulations, such as DRGs, have resulted in cost-shifting to outpatient areas of the health care sector and have not contained rising costs. The large number of uninsured individuals continue to plague the system.

Perhaps the proposed Dutch health care system may be the framework in which the optimal amount of quality, efficiency, equity, and cost containment can be achieved. It mandates univeral health care coverage. Instead of the employer-based system of the United States, it allows for individuals, regardless of job status, to select an insuring organization on the basis of cost containment and quality of care. Those insuring organizations that are more efficient or perceived to deliver higher quality health care will capture more business. The Dutch health care system attempts to eliminate competition to avoid high-risk individuals among insuring organizations. The case-mix adjusted cap, if set at an efficient level, will help contain those costs that far exceed the medical benefits to individuals. The proposed Dutch health care system will also help eliminate the losses in productivity of our current employer-based insurance as well as the inequities in paying for that insurance.

The proposed Dutch health care system points out vividly the choices that will have to be made to achieve quality, efficiency, equity, and cost containment in the American health care system. A system without a budget cap will involve ever-increasing health care costs, yet produce greater technological advances. A system that allows for more price competition will create more inequities. A system that seeks to eliminate competition based on risk selection will generate the need for more government regulation. A system that is based on choices between varying levels of price and quality will necessitate lower quality than when quality alone is considered. Clearly, competition, regulation, or rationing alone cannot achieve our goals. It will be the economists' (and society's) vital task to continue searching for the optimal policy mix.

References

Aaron, H. J., and Schwartz, W. B. (1984). *The Painful Prescription.* Washington, DC: The Brookings Institution.

Aaron, H. J., and Schwartz, W. B. (1990). "Rationing Health Care: The Choice Before Us," *Science* 247: 418–22.

Enthoven, A. (1978). "Consumer Choice Health Plan," *New England Journal of Medicine* 298 (nos. 12, 13): 650–58, 709–20.

———. (1988). "Managed Competition of Alternative Delivery Systems." In *Competition In the Health Care Sector: Ten Years Later,* W. Greenberg, ed., 83–99. Durham, NC: Duke University Press.

Evans, R. G. (1983). "Health Care in Canada: Patterns of Funding and Regulation," *Journal of Health Politics, Policy and Law* 8 (no. 1): 1–43.

Evans, R. G. et al. (1989). "Controlling Health Expenditures—the Canadian Reality," *The New England Journal of Medicine* 320 (no. 9): 571–77.

Iglehart, J. K. (1990). "Canada's Health Care System Faces Its Problems," *The New England Journal of Medicine* 322 (no. 8): 562–68.

International Communications Research (1990). *Excel Omnibus Study,* Table 4, page 4, December 7–11, 1990. Media, PA: ICR Survey Research Group.

Kirkman-Liff, B. L., and van de Ven, W. P. M. M.(1989). "Improving Efficiency in the Dutch Health Care System: Current Innovations and Future Options," *Health Policy* 13: 35–53.

Lapre, R. M. (1988). "A Change of Direction in the Dutch Health Care System?" *Health Policy* 10: 21–32.

Lister, J. (1989). "Proposals for Reform of the British National Health Service," *The New England Journal of Medicine* 320 (no. 13): 877–80.

Netherlands Ministry of Welfare, Health, and Cultural Affairs (1988). *Changing Health Care in the Netherlands.* The Hague, The Netherlands: Ministry of Welfare, Health, and Cultural Affairs.

Newhouse, J. P., Manning, W. G., Keeler, E. B., and Sloss, E. M. (1989). "Adjusting Capitation Rates Using Objective Health Resources and Prior Utilization," *Health Care Financing Review* 10: 41–54.

Schieber, G. J., and Pouillier, J. P. (1989). "Overview of International Comparisons of Health Care Expenditures," *Health Care Financing Review, Annual Supplement,* 1–7.

Schorr, A. L. (1990). "Job Turnover—A Problem with Employer-Based Health Care," *The New England Journal of Medicine* 323: 543–45.

Swartz, K. (1990). "Why Requiring Employers to Provide Health Insurance is a Bad Idea," *Journal of Health Politics, Policy and Law* 15 (no. 9): 779–92.

van de Ven, W. P. M. M. (1987). "The Key Role of Health Insurance in a Cost-Effective Health Care System," *Health Policy* 7: 253–72.

———. (1990). "From Regulated Cartel to Regulated Competition in the Dutch Health Care System," *European Economic Review* 34: 632–45.

———. (1991). "The Dutch Health Care System," paper presented at George Washington University, May 1991, Washington, DC.

van de Ven, W. P. M. M., and van Vliet, R. C. J. A. (1990). "How Can We Present Cream Skimming in a Competitive Health Insurance Market?" paper presented at the Second World Congress on Health Economics, September 1990, Zurich.

Index

About the Author

Warren Greenberg is Professor of Health Economics and of Health Care Sciences at the George Washington University. He is also Senior Fellow at the Center for Health Policy Research at George Washington. He has earned an international reputation on the subjects of competition and regulation in health care.

Dr. Greenberg received his B.A. in economics from Temple University, his M.A. in economics in 1965 from the University of Pennsylvania, and his Ph.D. in economics in 1972 from Bryn Mawr College. From 1971 until 1979, he was a staff economist with the Federal Trade Commission. He acted as lead economist for many of the commission's activities in the health care industry and was responsible for economic analysis of antitrust litigation.

Dr. Greenberg has served on review panels for the Health Care Financing Administration, the former National Center for Health Services Research, and the National Institute on Drug Abuse. He is a referee for many scholarly journals and is a member of the American Economic Association, the American Public Health Association, and the Association for Health Services Research.

Dr. Greenberg was Visiting Associate Professor of Managerial Economics at the University of Maryland in 1980 and 1981. In the fall of 1989, he was Visiting Professor at Ben-Gurion University in Israel. He continues his research on the Israeli and Dutch health care systems as well as on information dissemination; antitrust; and competition, regulation, and rationing in the U.S. health care sector. He is the author of numerous articles on the economics of health care and has edited or written nine books or monographs, including *Competition in the Health Care Sector: Past, Present and Future*; *Competition in the Health Care Sector: Ten Years Later*; and *Response to AIDS: Case Studies of HMO's, Insurers and Employers*.